Also by Peter Baxter:
*Rhodesia: Last Outpost of the British
Empire*
Selous Scouts (Africa@War Vol 4)

Co-published in 2011 by:

Helion & Company Limited
26 Willow Road
Solihull
West Midlands
B91 1UE
England
Tel. 0121 705 3393
Fax 0121 711 4075
email: info@helion.co.uk
website: www.helion.co.uk

and

30° South Publishers (Pty) Ltd.
16 Ivy Road
Pinetown 3610
South Africa
email: info@30degreessouth.co.za
website: www.30degreessouth.co.za

Text © Peter Baxter, 2011
Photographs © as individually credited

Designed & typeset by 30° South
Publishers (Pty) Ltd., South Africa
Cover design by 30° South Publishers
(Pty) Ltd., South Africa
Printed by Henry Ling Limited,
Dorchester, Dorset, UK
ISBN 978-1-907677-37-3

British Library Cataloguing-in-
Publication Data
A catalogue record for this book is
available from the British Library

Front cover photo: Yves Debay

CONTENTS

ABBREVIATIONS

APRD	*Armée Populaire pour la Restauration de la Démocratie*		GAPLC	*Groupe d'Action Patriotique pour la Libération de Centrafrique*
BONUCA	UN Peace-Building Office in the Central Africa		GPRF	*Gouvernement Provisoire de la République Française*
CAR	Central African Republic		MESAN	Movement for the Social Evolution of Black Africa
CCP	*Compagnie de Chasseurs Parachutistes*		MICOPAX	Mission for the Consolidation of Peace
CEMAC	Central African Economic and Monetary Union		MINURCA	*Mission des Nations Unies en Répulic Centrafricaine*
CEN-SAD	Community of Sahel Saharan States		MINURCAT	*Mission des Nations Unies en Répulic Centrafricaine et Tchad*
CFLN	*Comité Français de la Libération Nationale*		MISAB	*Mission Interafricaine de Surveillance des Accords de Bangui*
CPJP	Convention of Patriots for Justice and Peace		MLC	*Mouvement pour la Libération du Congo*
DGSE	*Direction Générale de la Sécurité Extérieur*		MLJC	*Mouvement des Libérateurs Centrafricains pour la Justice*
DRC	Democratic Republic of Congo		MPLC	Movement for the Liberation of the Central African People
ECCAS	Economic Community of Central African States		OAU	Organization of African Unity
EFAO	*Elements Français d'Assistance Operationelle*		RECAMP	*Capacités Africaines de Maintien de la Paix.*
EUFOR	European Union Force		RPIMa	*Régiment Parachutiste d'Infanterie de Marine*
FACA	*Forces Armées Centrafricaines*		SDECE	*Service de Documentation Extérieur et de Contre-Espionnage*
FDC	*Front Démocratique Centrafricain*		SPLA	Sudan People's Liberation Army
FDPC	*Forces pour la Démocratie du Peuple Centrafricain*		UFDR	*Union des Forces Démocratiques pour le Rassemblement*
FFCV	French Forces of Cape Verde		UN	United Nations
FFG	French Forces in Gabon		ZOM	*zone d'outre mer*
FLN	National Liberation Front (Algerian)			
FLNC	*Front de Libération Nationale Congolaise*			
FOMAC	*Forces Multinationales de Centrafrique*			
FOMUC	*Forces Multinationales de la CEMAC*			
FROLINAT	*Front de Libération Nationale du Tchad*			

CHAPTER ONE:
OUBANGUI-CHARI

"Once upon a time there was a landlocked French colony
in the very heart of Africa called Oubangui-Shari,
which was best known to the outside world for
supplying platter-lipped women to circus sideshows"
—*Washington Post*, 1977

Equatorial Africa is dominated by the wide and curving sweep of the Congo river. This iconic stream drains into the vast Congo Basin from the western slopes of the Great Rift Valley, from the central plateau of southern Africa and from a northward-probing finger known as the Ubangi river. This, the largest right-bank tributary of the Congo, draws from a watershed of some 600,000 square kilometres, encompassing a significant swathe of the northern frontier of the modern-day Democratic Republic of Congo, the southern Sudanese Bahr el-Ghazal and almost the entire area of the Central African Republic.

The Central African Republic, that problem child of Francophone Africa, was known to the French during the colonial period as the Oubangui-Chari. The Ubangui river marked the southern boundary and the Chari river the northern. In between lay a vast hinterland of absolute isolation; an unmapped landscape of riverine forest, wooded hill country and woodland savannah; a beautiful Eden, remote from the main fields of interest, sparsely populated, often unpopulated, a place of manifold wildlife—gorilla

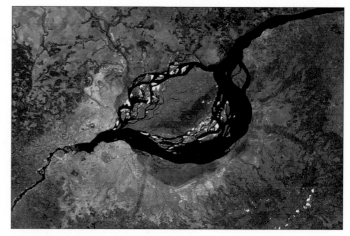

Satellite image of the Congo River Basin.
Source: Wikicommons

and rhinoceros, crocodile and lion—shielded from civilization by tsetse fly, and far beyond the crack of the slave trader's whip or the report of a hunter's rifle.

The territory was drawn into the French sphere of influence through the work of a certain Pierre Savorgnan de Brazza, the Italian-born doyen of French African exploration who, through his exploration of the river systems of Gabon, claimed some quarter of equatorial Africa for France. His great rival in this enterprise was the no less prominent Welsh/American explorer, Henry Morton Stanley, who, through a series of daring escapades,

Map of Oubangui-Chari, from a chocolate card printed *circa* 1910. *Source: Wikicommons*

staked *primum petere* to the Congo river itself, and by extension what hinterland he could reasonably include on behalf of the rapacious Belgian King Leopold II.

Such were the machinations of the 'scramble for Africa', the global-strategic partitioning of the continent that took place toward the end of the 19th century, and which by the turn of the next had seen Africa largely assigned to one or other of the great European powers. France and Britain, of course, dominated the game, but Belgium, Germany, Portugal, Italy and Spain worked hard to establish their own variously less significant spheres of influence.

For the French, de Brazza succeeded in staking out the entire right bank of the Congo river above the Stanley Pool, securing what in due course would become known as French Equatorial Africa. This vast region was subdivided into the administrative colonies of the French Congo, Gabon, Equatorial Guinea and the enormous interior expanse of Chad. A secondary effect of this was to block further international claim to any of the territories that could be reached via the navigable Ubangui river, or Oubangui river as it was better known, and any of its tributaries. Moreover it opened the theoretical possibility that the French could use this obvious highway into the interior to probe eastward into the Sudan and the Nile valley, possibly even extending French influence as far as the Indian Ocean. In this way French imperial interest would achieve some sort of geographic rationale between French North, West and Equatorial Africa, effectively straddling the continent all the way from the Gulf of Guinea to the Horn of Africa.

Such a scheme was enormously ambitious, but it was reflective of European imperial ambition in general, with each, to some degree or another manoeuvred to frustrate the ambitions of the other. Such was the 'Scramble for Africa'.

In the case of what was loosely defined as Haut-Oubangui, or Upper Oubangui, the river was explored by two brothers, Albert and Michel Dolisie, who in 1890 founded the settlement of Bangui below the rapids of the same name, marking the first substantive imperial imprint in the region. The territory that they encountered conformed more or less with the catchment of the upper reaches of Oubangui river and straddled three of the major ecological zones of Africa. Along the banks of the river itself a thick belt of tropical forest replicated the enervating conditions of the Congo, while farther north, on higher ground, the forests thinned out into expansive

Pierre Savorgnan de Brazza.
Source: Paul Nadar

Henry Morton Stanley.
Source: Wikicommons

King Leopold II of Belgium.
Source: Wikicommons

Captain Jean-Baptiste Marchand.
Source: Wikicommons

Fashoda: the governer's house, 1906.
Source: TIMEA

woodland savannah before conditions of severe aridity hinted at the proximity of the Sahara desert. It was a landscape of pristine beauty, largely untouched by the intrusion of outside religion or, indeed, the depredations of the slave trade, offering fertile soils, numerous rivers, a small population and almost limitless scope for industry and development.

Bangui consisted of a collection of mud and grass huts in a clearing that clung tenuously to the elbow of a river bend, linked to the outside world by river traffic, and isolated in the most profound way possible in a world rapidly developing industrial communications. However, by 1906, when the territory was formalized by the arrival of a French governor, it had developed into a quiet but pleasant colonial backwater. Bangui was designed with the usual arrangement of avenues radiating from a central administrative complex, and with a sufficient number of Europeans to allow for social diversion during the languid periods between journeys downriver to the main administrative centre of Brazzaville. Here the governor-general of French Equatorial Africa managed the vast territories under his remit, including the Upper Bangui, which by 1910 was known as Oubangu-Chari.[1]

The indigenous population that found itself under French

colonial domination numbered about a million and consisted of those groups representative of the climatic zones of the territory. The principal ethnic distinctions then, as today, are, east to west, the Banda and the Baya ethnic groups, both tending to be concentrated along the banks of the Ubangi river, and both to a greater or lesser extent owing their cultural origins to the Bantu speakers of the Niger–Congo region. The Baya, however, are the more numerous of the two, averaging some 35 per cent of the local population, and are speakers of one or other of the Ubangian languages that are more closely associated with direct regional dialects.

Among the Ubangian speakers were the M'Baka minority, a Bantu people located in the densely forested and heavily populated southwestern districts centred around the current city of Boda. The M'Baka were then, and remain today, a resolute, intelligent and resourceful sub-group within the general population and who remain, as they were then, disproportionately represented in government, business and the arts.

In the meanwhile, in 1896, a French military column left Gabon and set off inland with the objective of driving the equatorial African conquests of the Third Republic east. Specific instructions required the expedition to seize the Upper Nile in the name of France, and if possible link up with the Emperor Menelik in Abyssinia. The complement of force assigned to this expedition consisted of twelve European personnel, a detail of 150 native infantry and some 13,500 African porters. The expedition was commanded by the redoubtable Captain Jean-Baptiste Marchand, by then a veteran of several similar expeditions, including among them an earlier exploration of the sources of the Niger river.

After an extraordinary fourteen-month combined river and overland journey, Marchand's expedition reached the abandoned fort of Fashoda on the Nile river, in July 1898. There, in what was widely regarded as the British sphere of influence, he hoped to rendezvous with a second French expedition that had earlier set out for the same point from Djibouti on the Red Sea. Unfortunately this expedition had already arrived in Fashoda and, finding no trace of Marchand, had made the assumption that he had either perished or returned, and thus it had itself turned around.

The British, of course, were aware of all of this, even contemplating at one time the dispatch of a military expedition from Uganda to intervene. However, it was fortunate at that moment that Lord Kitchener, in command of an Anglo–Egyptian army fresh from victory at Omdurman, was available locally to respond. On 11 September 1898, Kitchener arrived at Fashoda on board a flotilla of five steamers carrying two battalions of Sudanese, one hundred Cameron Highlanders, a battery of artillery and four Maxim guns.

This immediately precipitated an international crisis. France, it seemed, was prepared to back the legitimacy of the expedition to the point of war with Britain. Kitchener, however, and in a manner somewhat out of character, dealt with the matter sympathetically and cautiously, recognizing no doubt in Marchand a man of character and determination who was caught somewhat on the

---

[1] Chari is the name of a river which empties into Lake Chad, the headwaters of which, under various names, partly delimits the Central African Republic to the north.

The last picture of Lord Kitchener, seen here leaving Westminster from a meeting with MPs.
Source: Illustrated London News

The Battle of Omdurman.
Source: Wikicommons

horns of a dilemma. It was soon agreed between the two that matters on the ground could best remain static with the issue left to the metropolitan powers to resolve. Kitchener, therefore, established a garrison alongside the French, hoisted the Egyptian flag (avoiding any inflammatory temptation to hoist the Union Jack) and shortly after left the scene.

Meanwhile, in Europe a diplomatic war was being fought between London and Paris with the usual jingoistic verbiage of the times flowing back and forth across the English Channel. That British Prime Minister Lord Salisbury should have applied such thoroughly British understatement as to describe Marchand as "an explorer in difficulties on the Upper Nile" incensed the French, who replied that this was simply another instance of British greed and bullying.[1] It did not help at all to be reminded that had the British not defeated the Mahdists at Omdurman, the likelihood was that the French would have been wiped out at Fashoda by the Sudanese themselves.

On this occasion, however, the French were quite clearly outgunned, both militarily and diplomatically, and despite the intense furore raging on the European mainland, Marchand learned on a trip to Cairo, and to his unutterable disgust, that the French were backing down. The French military at home was already divided over the Dreyfus espionage affair and could not reasonably be expected to challenge a mighty and united British and allied army. It had nonetheless been a close-run thing. At a banquet held in London in honour of Lord Kitchener, the Lord Mayor was able to announce that the crisis was over and that the French were willing to withdraw.

March 1899 saw the signing in London of an agreement that confirmed the Nile valley as an Anglo–Egyptian preserve, leaving the French with a free hand west of the river. Later that month an agreement was signed between the British and Egyptians by which the Sudan would be governed by a dual mandate between the two powers, with Charles Gordon serving as governor-general.

Thus French Equatorial Africa was introduced to the eastern limit of its expansion; the territory of Oubangu-Chari, instead of becoming the strategic platform for this eastward advance, turned out to be what many would describe as a colonial *cul-de-sac*, remaining a languid and distant imperial backwater and indeed, into the future, the impoverished problem child of the French colonial family.

By the turn of the century, the colonial boundaries of Africa had been more or less established, which brought an end to the competition for territory that had characterized the 'Scramble' and introduced a more settled period of sustained exploitation. As was popular at the time across the entire colonial spectrum, the utilization of remote and unattractive territories was usually conducted by commercial companies. These would typically be

Lord Salisbury, 1889.
Source: Blue and Old Gold

A Marseille newspaper declares Dreyfus innocent.
Source: Wikicommons

Compagnie Forestière de la
Sangha-Oubangui.
Source: Wikicommons

Jean-Bédel Bokassa while serving
in the Foreign Legion,1939.
Source: Wikicommons

in possession of sizeable land grants or leases, sometimes entire territories, where they would operate a variety of businesses from plantations and estates to trading, transport and construction. The tradition of chartered companies can be traced back to the early coastal trade in slaves and raw materials that set in motion the process of colonization, and which were often continued once the Europeans made substantive landfall and began to penetrate inland in search of fresh resources and opportunity.

In some of the better publicized and more central colonies, such as Côte d'Ivoire, Gabon, French Congo and Senegal, these companies were often well capitalized and very successful. In other territories, such as Oubangu-Chari, they were less so. Consequently the *capito* culture of *petit bourgeois* overlordship that characterized all the European colonies in one form or another was of a much lower standard here, and the natives who fell under such under-regulated and exploitative regimes suffered accordingly.

Oubangu-Chari was officially recognized as a colony in 1903 and given its own governor three years later. By then it was estimated that over half the entire territory was administered more or less independently by seventeen individual companies. The global rubber boom that occurred at the turn of the century introduced a frenzy of economic activity in the equatorial colonies of Brazil, the East Indies and Equatorial Africa. Excesses of zeal in encouraging production were highlighted in the Belgian Congo during this period, but many similar excesses were permitted elsewhere, in particular where public scrutiny was less glaring and where the recruitment of European administrative staff less selective.

Perhaps the most notorious of these local consortia was the Compagnie Forestière de la Sangha-Oubangui, engaged in the collection of rubber in the district of Lobaye. The system at the time required local communities to contribute rubber from the wild harvest, at times exacting it as a form of taxation, at others

engaging in forced recruitment by the application of a number of none too gentle methods. Sometimes women and children were held hostage, released only upon the fulfilment of family quotas; at others simpler methods of floggings, beatings or mutilation and death applied as a salutary indication to others of the consequences of non-cooperation. It has been estimated, perhaps fancifully, but perhaps not, that between 1890 and 1940 half the population of the territory perished from a combination of microbial shock and colonial violence.[2]

The recorded examples of institutionalized brutality in the colony are indeed many. It can be understood to a degree when it is considered that by the turn of the 19th century less than two hundred European expatriates were responsible for controlling and keeping more than a million natives in order.[3] It is also a fact, as already mentioned, that such a remote, unimportant and administratively weak colony as Oubangu-Chari could hardly be expected to attract the cream of the expatriate crop.

A particularly lurid and impactful record of this sort of arbitrary violence at the hands of agents of the Compagnie Forestière de la Sangha-Oubangui was made as late as 1927, in the prefecture of Lobaye, with the brutal doing to death of a recalcitrant local headman by the name of Mindogon Ngboundoulou. The backdrop of this incident was a localized uprising by Baya tribesmen north of Lobaye. Disturbances were centred around a prophet called Karnu who issued a widely heeded call to resist French rule and forced labour. This was the most significant peasant uprising within French colonial territory to date and was suppressed only with great difficulty. Although the M'Baka of the Lobaye district did not rise up to quite the same extent, an uncommon resistance was nonetheless noticeable to the white company administration, who then thought it necessary to impress upon the surrounding villages certain blunt realities.

The opportunity arose in November 1927 when Mindogon Ngboundoulou took it upon himself to release from captivity a number of hostages being held by the Forestière as a guarantee that their relatives would work. This was immediately construed as an act of rebellion, upon which Mindogon Ngboundoulou was arrested. He was produced on the morning of 13 November in the public square of the Mbaïki Prefecture, where he was bound hand and foot and methodically beaten to death.

The singular brutality of this incident resonated through the community, achieving in the short term the required effect of pacifying the rebellion, but also embedding within the community an enduring suspicion and hatred for the forces of colonization. Within the family of the executed man, the effect was more profound. His wife, Marie Yokowo, proved to have been so traumatized by the sight of her husband's killing that she committed suicide some two weeks later. Behind remained a brood of orphans now taken in by their grandparents. Significantly, one of these was a six-year-old by the name of Jean Bokassa.

Soldiers of the Lincolnshire Regiment photographed during a lull in the fighting at the Battle of Omdurman, 2 September 1898. *Source: Wikicommons*

A romanticized illustration of the Battle of Omdurman, 2 September 1898. *Source: Wikicommons*

SS *Tacoma* burns after being hit by British naval shellfire, 24 September 1940. *Source: Wikicommons*

A Vichy French destroyer in action, Dakar Harbour, 24 September 1940. *Source: Wikicommons*

CHAPTER TWO:
THE BIRTH OF A TYRANT

In later years Jean-Bédel Bokassa was apt to describe the killing of his father with certain embellishments. For instance he stated on more than one occasion that the *coup de grâce* had been delivered by means of a nail driven into his father's head, which was cheaper than a bullet. Such creativity in matters of violence are perhaps revealing of a substrata of the mind of a man affected by the kind of institutionalized violence that he was weaned upon, and which on many occasions as a child he watched being applied by those that had thoroughly mastered it.

Bokassa was born on 22 February 1921 in the large M'Baka village of Bobangui, situated in the southeast of the country on the edge of the equatorial rainforest, and some eighty kilometres distant from the capital. This was the heartland of the rubber industry and one of the wealthier and more developed prefectures of the colony. It was thanks to this that Bokassa's grandparents were able to contemplate the education of some, among the many, grandchildren now under their care. Jean Bokassa was chosen from among them to receive a French-language education at the Catholic mission school of École Sainte-Jeanne d'Arc, situated in Mbaïki, and one of the few mission schools in the territory.

As a child Bokassa was shorter than average, and having suffered the ignominy of his father's execution and his mother's suicide, he endured frequent taunts that he learned to deal with, or at least silence, with violence. He may have been undersized but he was fit, well proportioned and strong; although not academically brilliant he was competent and interested, and in fact took for himself the name Bédel from the well-known author of a book on French grammar. An early suggestion that he might enter the priesthood was disabused before too long thanks to a conspicuous lack of piety, after which Bokassa went on to continue his education at the École Saint-Louis in Bangui, followed by finishing in Brazzaville where, among other skills, he learned to cook.

The army then beckoned as an obvious career choice. Upon his graduation in 1939, on the eve of the Second World War, he joined the French army as a private. In this regard Bokassa was among many thousands of black Africans originating from the French African colonies to volunteer for military service with the French. He was inducted into the 2nd Bataillon de Marche, a French Equatorial African unit specific to Oubangui-Chari that was integrated with the Free French Forces of de Gaulle after the fall of Paris and the rise of Vichy. It was also, incidentally, the first unit of the French army to receive the Cross of the Order of Liberation on 9 September 1942.

Bokassa, then an 18-year-old youth, found in the army a home very much to his liking. In July 1940, he was promoted to corporal and a year later sergeant. He saw action in Operation *Dragoon*, the August 1944 Allied landings on the coast of Provence, remaining in Germany as part of the Allied occupation force until the end of

Charles de Gaulle.
Source: Divide and Conquer

General de Gaulle salutes outside the summer palace of the Bey of Tunis, June 1943
Source: Divide and Conquer

the war. Thereafter he remained both in France and in uniform, stationed at the army camp at Fréjus on the French Riviera. There he studied signals and radio communications, earning himself a place at the French officer training school at Saint-Louis du Sénégal in Senegal.

In September 1950, Bokassa left for Indochina as transmissions expert with the colonial battalion of Saigon-Cholon. Here again he saw considerable action, receiving a number of minor wounds, and adding to a total of twelve citations for bravery, a membership of Legion d'Honneur, the Médaille Militaire and the Croix de Guerre. He was broadly recognized by his officers as an excellent soldier of the ranks, and indeed as a fighting platoon or company officer—he was promoted to lieutenant in 1958 and captain in 1961—but he was also noted as being capricious, vain and self-opinionated.

Bokassa's term of service in Indochina also revealed a rapacious interest in women that resulted in numerous affairs, including one with a 17-year-old Vietnamese girl named Nguyen Thi Hué, who bore him a daughter and whom he later married. However, upon the completion of his tour of duty in 1953, he left his new family in Saigon, believing that he would return for further service before too long. This, however, he did not, and he soon lost contact with the child and her mother.

In the meanwhile, Bokassa returned to Fréjus where he served as a transmissions instructor to African recruits, before being posted as a military technical assistant in Brazzaville, and in 1959 to Bangui, returning to his homeland after a twenty-year absence.

In those two decades a great deal had happened in the world, and the complexion of both the major European powers and their overseas territories had radically changed. In fact, the summer of 1958 was particularly eventful both for France and

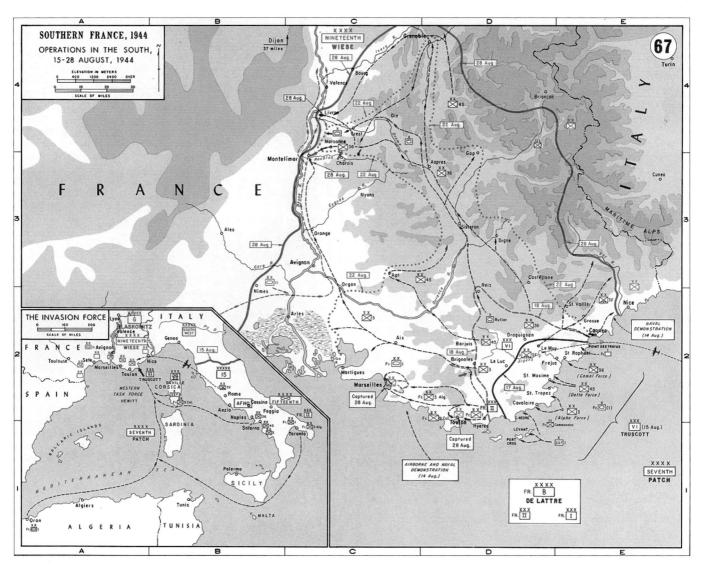

Operation *Dragoon*.
Source: Wikicommons

her overseas empire. When the news reached him of de Gaulle's election as prime minister of France, Bokassa was on attachment in Brazzaville. This was a significant moment for a lowly black officer in a French regiment. De Gaulle had led the Free French in a resistance to the German occupation of the mainland with a degree of determination and integrity that had rendered him a hero in the eyes of many, not least among them the many African servicemen who had fought alongside the Free French in Africa and Europe.

It was de Gaulle, perhaps more than any other French leader before or since, who appreciated and attempted to preserve the unique interdependence of metropolitan France and her black African possessions. Indeed it was the contribution of black Africa to the French struggle during two world wars, in particular the first, that embedded in his mind and in the minds of many, the unique importance of this region to the French sense of her own global destiny.

The French style of African colonization was different in many ways to the British, that other great European influence on the continent. The French were often regarded as wielding the iron fist more frequently and more deliberately in Africa than ever done by the British, but at the same time a far greater willingness to nurture and absorb indigenous talent was evident in French colonialism. This was particularly the case in military *entente* that allowed men like Bokassa to serve in the French army, and to achieve levels of rank and distinction that would have been inconceivable to a black man in any of the British or allied native regiments. French influence and military reach in Africa is greater today than any other ex-colonial power and this is thanks almost entirely to the fact that the African elite was afforded access to the defining processes. In the aftermath of the Second World War, France was able to reclaim its place among the great global powers because it had managed to retain its empire, and equally, to those under its dominion in Africa, it was the share that they were offered of French grandeur and independence that elevated them to a special status.[4]

And many among them believed this, for in many ways it was true. To this day decisions in Francophone Africa are taken at the highest level with the possible reaction of France in mind. French military cooperation with Africa exceeds that of any nation outside the continent, and the careful integration of the French army with the many *armées nationales* with which she has cooperated since independence ensures a continuation of that cooperation. A French soldier can with immediacy slip into a functional role in any one

Berlin Conference to carve up Africa among the European powers.
Source: Wikicommons

General Buhrer.
Source: Wikicommons

Edouard Daladier.
Source: Wikicommons

of many Francophone armies in Africa, quite as an African soldier might be welcomed into the ranks and into the academies of the French military establishment. All this is the careful cultivation of the French self image and the determination that French prestige, configured so closely to the success of her post-imperial relationship with Africa, continues.

The French Empire, or *France Outre-Mer* (overseas), came into being along the lines defined by the Berlin Conference of 1884/5, and did not differ appreciably from the geo-strategic aims and ambitions of other European powers. It was in the late 1930s, however, that politicians and military planners began making increased reference to the overseas territories and the French *mission civilisatrice*.

Gaston Monnerville.
Source: Wikicommons

Military planners also began to take greater account of the twin factors of what aid the empire could provide for France in the advent of war, and what dangers the empire might face as a consequence of war. Germany, after all, had been stripped of her overseas empire on her defeat in 1918, and no doubt Hitler, in his demands for the restoration of the German empire, would sanction the Allies in this regard as heavily as Germany had been sanctioned, should Germany win the war. The proclamation by General Buhrer, Chief of the French Colonial General Staff, that the empire could provide up to six million men in the event of war, was obviously wildly exaggerated, but the idea that the empire represented an enormous reservoir of men added significant value to the existence of the overseas territories. According to President Edouard Daladier:

> The French Force? It is present in the whole world. It is the measure of this immense Empire which is the African bloc, intangible, yet a type of central armour, whose affectionate attachment to the mother country I myself was recently able to measure.[5]

Paul Giacobbi.
Source: Wikicommons

In the event, black Africa was divided. Cameroon and all of French Equatorial Africa, with the exception of Gabon, and including Oubangui-Chari, joined the Free French, while the remaining territories declared for Vichy. Between July and November 1940, Free French forces battled troops loyal to Vichy in two battles on French West African soil. These, known as the West Africa Campaign, were the Battle of Dakar, also known as Opération *Menace*, and the Battle of Gabon. The result was inconclusive, with the Vichy French claiming victory at the Battle of Dakar and the Free French claiming victory at the Battle of Gabon. French Equatorial Africa, however, remained in Free French hands while French West Africa was claimed by Vichy.

Ultimately nearly 200,000 black Africans were mobilized in the service of France during the Second World War.

Many of the loyalties first committed to Vichy in black Africa were revised upon consideration, and transferred to de Gaulle and the Free French. Félix Eboué, for example, the black, French Guiana-born governor of Chad, declared initially for Vichy but on 26 June 1940 for de Gaulle. Similar action was quickly followed by Cameroon, Middle Congo and Obangui-Chari.

Governor Georges Pierre Masson of Gabon, as we have heard, chose to remain loyal to Pétain, but in November 1940, Free French troops successfully landed in Gabon. The territory was then claimed by de Gaulle and Masson committed suicide. Senegal did not follow suit until the Allied

Léopold Sédar Senghor.
Source: Wikicommons

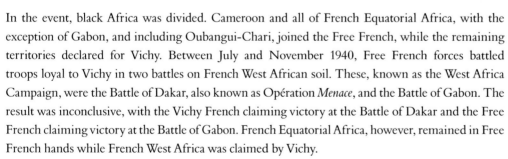

Félix Houphouët-Boigny.
Source: Wikicommons

Barthélémy Boganda.
Source: Wikicommons

Ahmed Sékou Touré.
Source: Wikicommons

David Dacko.
Source: Wikicommons

landings in North Africa took place on 8 November 1942. By the time Axis troops evacuated Tunisia on 13 May 1943, all of French Africa was more or less committed to the Free French.

In 1943 de Gaulle was able to establish the *Comité Français de la Libération Nationale*, or CFLN, in Algiers, which later became the provisional government of the French Republic, or *Gouvernement Provisoire de la République Française*, the GPRF.

Thus it is evident that during the war Vichy and Free France competed for favour in Africa, and the ebb and flow of this struggle directly affected the bitter power struggles within and for France itself during those dark days.

De Gaulle's eventual victory in securing black Africa to his cause offered final vindication of the value of overseas power in securing France's position in Europe. French Guianan lawyer and politician, Gaston, made a succinct point in 1945 when he remarked: "Without Empire France today would only be a liberated country. Thanks to her Empire it is today a victorious country."[6] This was added to in a post mortem of events by the French minister of the colonies, Paul Giacobbi, who spoke in August 1945:

> During the war that has just ended it was in the Empire that French liberty survived, it was by the Empire that France constantly persevered in the struggle, it is from the Empire that the French forces of liberation were launched.[7]

All this served to cement the view across the social and political spectrum that for France to remain a European power it was imperative that she also remain an imperial power, and most particularly an African imperial power. It was thanks in large part to this sense of imperial destiny, indeed of imperial imperative, that France endeavoured at such economic, political and military cost to retain control of *France Outre-Mer*.

One of Charles de Gaulle's first actions upon taking the office of Prime Minister, and shortly after as President of the Republic, was to implement a new constitution that would allow for autonomous 'colonies' to claim a place as members of a French Union. Years of emotional debate had preceded this first deliberate step toward the devolution of the empire. Many eminent thinkers and policymakers contributed to it, but perhaps none so eloquently as Léopold Sédar Senghor.

A poet, politician and cultural theorist, Senghor typified the ideal of the black African elite that the French saw as the first generation of indigenous leaders in a post-imperial world. Senghor was the first African to be elected as a member of the French Academy, an *alumnus* of the Sorbonne and the University of Paris and arguably one of the most important black African intellectuals of the 20th century. The essence of his view was that, once the more destructive features of both European imperialism and black nationalism had been curbed, each could join in a natural and equal polarity. "The Europe that must be created does not stop in Marseilles or Sicily," Senghor remarked, "... it is in reality two continents which are complimentary, that is Europe and Africa, in reality it is a political, economic and cultural Eurafrican community which must be formed."

Many similar contributions were made to the debate, some emotive, others fanciful, and yet others eminently sensible, but it was one man, Charles de Gaulle, who ultimately managed the transition, and who defined its practical parameters. His sense of the future was informed by the recent past, and by the role that Africa had played in supporting the Free French. The general post-war feeling that France was to Africa what Sampson was to his hair, was to de Gaulle a matter of fact, not legend. However, external factors—the expectations of the Atlantic Charter, the wars in Algeria and Indochina and a general shift in the global power equation—tended to impose an agenda on de Gaulle that was not always to his taste. However, decolonization, in the manner being undertaken by the British—what many French, and indeed many British colonists regarded as an ignominious retreat from the continent based on a profound disbelief in the continuing capacity of the British Empire to function—was not the pattern that either de Gaulle or France wished to follow.

In the post-war period, in that superb hiatus between the stirring of the black masses from their thousand-year sleep and their violent awakening covering the two decades after 1945, the French considered simply the redrafting of the original imperial design, not a renunciation of it. The French Union, in its infant form, was established by *Title Eight* of the new French Constitution of October 13, 1946, that gave birth to the Fourth Republic.

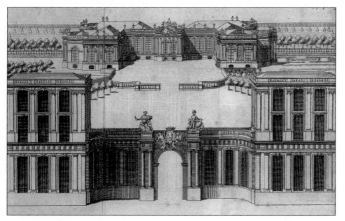

The Palais Bourbon.
Source: Wikicommons

The preamble stated that "France together with the overseas peoples shall form a union founded upon equality of rights and duties, without distinction of race or religion". This moderate language was obscured by the more detailed articles that followed, which tended to define differing standards of membership in the union, all of which served generally to ensure the durability of France's past colonial legacy.

Pressure to revise the forms of overseas control envisaged by the French came primarily from the *évolués* class of black: the Senghors of the French colonial system; those that were a source of such pride and irritation. But it was here that the beauty of the French system lay. It was the elite among the blacks, who had achieved their elitism through exposure to metropolitan France and who had so much to gain by maintaining that contact, who would drive change from within. They were seated in the French Assembly, so better them than the warlords and revolutionaries.

Ivorian Félix Houphouët-Boigny was the first among equals in this club. A landowner and a Christian parent, he was hardly the one to be waging war with France. Perhaps one of his most memorable comments in the matter of black self-determination was uttered at the 1958 opening of a trade fair in Côte d'Ivoire. "If you don't want to vegetate in bamboo huts,' he said, "concentrate your efforts on growing good cocoa and coffee."

In 1946, Houphouët-Boigny was forty-one years old. He was a native of Côte d'Ivoire, of high birth and educated initially by the colonial administration itself. He later qualified with a medical degree from the French West Africa School of Medicine in Senegal. Thereafter he entered politics at a village, and then municipal level, edging through the first cracks that were opening in the tightly ethnocentric system being created by the birth of the French Union.

The constitution of the Fourth Republic, representing perhaps the largest of those cracks, and which had been adopted by referendum in October 1946, allowed for colonial representation in both houses of parliament: seven per cent of the seats of the National Assembly and fifteen per cent of those in the Council of the Republic. In addition, all the colonies were given limited indigenous authority through the formation of local assemblies that were empowered to debate and approve local budget items. A double-college system governing elections overseas was also introduced, with one college for French expatriates and another for native people, albeit with the indigenous franchise limited to a tiny educated elite. Furthermore, colonies were no longer referred to by that name, but as *territoires d'outre-mer*, or overseas territories.

In due course Félix Houphouët-Boigny found himself occupying a seat in the Palais Bourbon. Close by him sat Léopold Sédar Senghor of Senegal. The two were political rivals, of course, but united in their general conservatism. Both were members of the tiny, French-educated and intellectually forceful elite, occupying their seats in the National Assembly of the Fourth Republic as nothing less than equals, and by this serving fair notice of the fact that they were destined to govern their respective territories sooner rather than later.

So much for the apprentices. The master, President Charles de Gaulle, was charged with the responsibility of making it all work. While the British Empire was devolving into a commonwealth, de Gaulle pictured a modern federal state that would include, as overseas members, France's African territories.

In essence de Gaulle put it to the crop of French African dependencies, now all looking on with anxious expectation to be told by *le Général* how the future would look, that two avenues of progress were open to them. The first was membership of the new French global union, or federation, along with which would come all the benefits of French political and economic patronage. The second was total independence, the rewards for which would be a severing of all links with France—social, political and military, and most importantly, economically. "But what is inconceivable," de Gaulle said in a press interview on the matter, "is an independent state which France continues to help. If the choice is for independence, the government will draw, with regret, the conclusions that follow from the expression of that choice."[8]

In the meanwhile, sharing a seat at the Assembly with the likes of Houphouët-Boigny and Sédar Senghor was another of the emerging political elite, Oubangui-Chari's Barthélémy Boganda. Boganda's route to prominence had been another common avenue of native advancement: the church. He was the first black Catholic priest to be ordained in the central African territory, and like Jean-Bédel Bokassa, to whom he was distantly related, he was of the M'Baka tribe. He founded and led the first substantive indigenous political organization, the Movement for the Social Evolution of Black Africa or MESAN, which was less than a political party, but somewhat more than a pressure group. Like Bokassa again, he was mission-educated. And in common with most black politicians of his era, his objective was not necessarily independence from France, but better treatment for blacks within the institutions of colonial government.

Oubangui-Chari, however, was neither Côte d'Ivoire nor Senegal. Even this call for limited reform within the territory kindled the ire of the local French administration, and even more so the still-powerful companies that traded in cotton, coffee, diamonds and other commodities. The discontinuation of forced labour in the territory was a recent and somewhat radical policy decision that was seen by many irritated expatriates as being

Quai d'Orsay.
Source: Wikicommons

directly attributable to the emergence of black nationalism. Black political activity was by its nature left-leaning, and as such a threat to the hallowed principles of free-enterprise. It also broke a traditional convention of non-interference on the part of the metropolitan government in the minor points of the commercial administration of the colony.

In the meanwhile, the French legislative session of 1957 saw the introduction of fresh reforms under the *loi-cadre*, or legal framework of the new *France d'Outre-Mer*. Universal suffrage replaced the double-college franchise, substantive power was devolved to the territorial assemblies; although French governors retained the title, and to a considerable degree, the powers of a president. On the fringes, however, vice-presidents, those being the most senior elected black representatives in each territory, were able to amass significant political influence. However, by mid-1958 the power balance in the overseas territories was seen to be tipping steeply in the favour of local representation. It was thereafter that territorial governors became increasing titular, while real administrative authority lay increasingly in the hands of local elected officials.

The new legal framework also allowed for the election of 'great councils' to preside over the two federal amalgamations of French West Africa and French Equatorial Africa. Ivorian leader Félix Houphouët-Boigny presided over the former and Barthélémy Boganda the latter. With this Boganda hoped to lead the confederation of French Equatorial Africa to independence as a united territory under the name of the Central African Republic.

It was at this moment that Charles de Gaulle took up the reins of government as president of the Fifth Republic, and the point at which the offer of unconditional but unsupported independence was made to any territory that should choose it. A constitutional referendum held in October 1958 revealed that only the territory of Guinea, led by the firebrand nationalist Ahmed Sékou Touré, was willing to venture into statehood unassisted. The French responded to this with stone-faced Gallic formality, removing all official personnel and everything of value to the new republic, serving notice on others observing from the wings that what de

Gaulle said was what de Gaulle meant. The message was absorbed, and although some caution crept into the language of liberation thereafter, the slow march toward it continued.

Barthélémy Boganda's dream of a greater Central African Republic, however, foundered on the unwillingness of individual territorial leaders to contemplate the status of a deputy in a federal assembly, rather than a president, a bounty which for all was guaranteed at a distinctly discernable point in the near future. Thus, when the Central Africa Republic was founded as a member of the French Union, it did so with the same basic territorial delineations as had existed before. It was still, however, little more than a colonial *cul-de-sac*.

Tragedy would now thwart Boganda's destiny to lead his republic to independence. On 29 March 1959, he boarded an aircraft for the short flight from the town of Berbérati to Bangui, but he never arrived. His aircraft exploded in mid air, killing him and everyone else on board. Sabotage was widely suspected but never proven, although the Paris weekly, *L'Express*, published a report that traces of explosive had been found in the wreckage. It was widely held that a conspiracy of local French businessmen and the French secret service had orchestrated an assassination.

Boganda was succeeded as prime minister by socialist academic Abel Goumba, but as president-apparent of an independent republic, Goumba's place was taken by another M'Baka, a school teacher by the name of David Dacko. Elected initially to a seat in the territorial assembly, Dacko was an early supporter of Boganda, and served in his government in a variety of portfolios, including the interior, commerce and the economy ministries. However, the main engine of his rise to political contention was the support of the local French commercial and administrative community, and the Quai d'Orsay itself. Goumba was suspected by both to have been too left leaning and too nationalistic. It can be seen, therefore, that despite handing the mechanisms of power over to blacks, France conspired throughout to retain, through economic leverage, as much influence as it could.

In the meanwhile, and in a sign of things to come, Dacko, secure in the backing of France, influenced the vote by surrounding parliament with his own militia, in this case a small army of arrow-wielding pygmies, after which, by way of a reward for council votes, a no-questions-asked extension to the parliamentary term of office was confirmed for all. Thus, on 13 August 1960, the Central African Republic gained independence, and David Dacko was duly elected to the presidency. Soon after, and in a further sign of things to come, Abel Goumba and his key clique of supporters found themselves under arrest. In July 1962 Dacko instituted a one-party state, followed by a statutory requirement that all adults be fee-paying members of MESAN. Needless to say, at the 1964 general election, David Dacko was delighted to record 100 per cent of the popular vote.

As all this was taking place, Jean-Bédel Bokassa remained on attachment with the French army in Bangui, somewhat remote from the power play taking place, but nonetheless a deeply interested observer. He was able to predict with some confidence, being as he belonged to that educated elite for whom the gates of the banquet were being thrown wide, that he would find some role among the state bourgeoisie that would be both lucrative and powerful. It also bears mentioning that he was a cousin of David Dacko, for the sake of current political significance, and a nephew of Barthélemy Boganda, for what symbolic gravitas that could provide.

On 1 January 1962, Bokassa bade farewell to the French army and committed himself to the military forces of the CAR with the rank of battalion commandant. His immediate task was to form the new military, and a little over a year later he was duly appointed commander-in-chief of an extremely modest 500-man *Forces Armées Centrafricaines*, or FACA. Thanks to his relationship to Dacko, but perhaps more importantly, to the experience that he had acquired abroad in the French army, Bokassa was able to rise swiftly through the ranks, becoming chief of staff and the Central African army's first colonel on 1 December 1964.

Most historians would agree that the developing tragedy of the Central African Republic began at this moment. From his vantage at the head of the armed forces, Bokassa was able to observe the evolution of indigenous political process. The preferred polarity of a one party state had already by then become something of a pattern in black Africa. 'One-man-one-vote ... once' tended to be the derisive assessment of most whites as they pondered the black man settling into power. And indeed this was depressingly often, in fact almost universally, the case. That a nibbling at the edges of the bounty of state very quickly degenerated into wholesale corruption also tended to follow by then a well-worn pattern.

The system of patronage, for observers of a charitable disposition, was seen, and explained, as being deeply embedded and intrinsically African, and something that could not be thrown off, as whites tended to expect, within a single political generation. Indeed, the first indigenous politicians to govern the country were those that had been educated thanks to sacrifices made by poorer family members, all of whom now stood in line for what was due to them.

If Bokassa felt some outrage at this pattern, and he did, it was not because of any anger at the degeneration of the state into a pool of parasitic functionaries, but simply the fact the he was not getting fat enough, quickly enough, himself.

From this root it is not difficult to picture how the tree of Bokassa's absolute self-absorption began to grow. He was not brilliantly educated—certainly he was no Senghor—but he could read and write, but perhaps more importantly he had travelled, and had been exposed to, and was somewhat wise in the ways of, the world. He was also possessed of a common touch and a certain charm and charisma. This, in combination with a childlike and unrestrained cupidity, qualified him as an almost perfect candidate for power in the emerging political landscape of black Africa.

Bokassa initially attempted to achieve recognition in government by insinuating himself into Dacko's inner circle, manoeuvres that at times had about them an almost comical ignorance of protocol.

Dacko tended to be dismissive of his efforts, and on one occasion insulted Bokassa with the comment before a large gathering of French and local dignitaries that Bokassa was a simple medal collector and rather too stupid to stage a coup.

The realization that he had dangerously underestimated his cousin was reached by Dacko shortly afterward, but it came too late to avert the inevitable. By then black African governments across the continent were toppling to military coups, and with Bokassa placed at the head of the army, there was an almost depressing certainty that he too would soon seize this fast-track route to power.

Indeed, on the morning of New Year, 1966, the world at large awoke to the news that yet another obscure African country had fallen to a coup d'état. In the event David Dacko tried to take action to avert it but he acted too late. He first tried to exile Bokassa to France, then he attempted to manipulate the budget to strengthen the gendarmerie and weaken the army, and finally he resolved to replace Bokassa at the head of the army. He was indiscreet enough, however, to mention this fact here and there, whisperings of which very quickly reached Bokassa. On the evening of 31 December 1965, the president left Bangui to visit the estate of one of his ministers, and it was then that Bokassa played his hand.

The coup was a success; the French, of course, made certain of this by, if not openly supporting Bokassa, then at least by not supporting Dacko. The French had concluded by then that Dacko had slipped out of alignment and was not quite the friend that he had at first promised to be. A man like Bokassa, unbalanced as he might appear, was nonetheless an *alumnus* of the French military, and a Francophile of the most passionate sort. Dacko was arrested, and in due course found himself taking his turn in the notorious Ngaragba prison. That he was not immediately killed was due to the risk this would pose to French aid, and indeed he would survive the bloodshed to later serve as an adviser to Bokassa.

So it was. Bokassa greeted 1966 in a self-congratulatory mood. He had not slept, of course, but a new dawn crept over the capital that to him seemed rich with golden promise. A few formalities, such as Dacko's written resignation, were required, but beyond that the gates of the republic had been thrown wide open, and Bokassa walked through with some small part of his ambition satisfied, but only a small part.

Had there ever been one prepared, a psychiatric report of Jean-Bédel Bokassa would have made fascinating reading. Whether or not he modelled the phases of his life on Napoleon Bonaparte is a matter of conjecture, but the fact that his life, in a more modest version, followed a very similar course is inescapable. The spirit of Napoleon, one would suppose reluctantly conjured, remained juxtaposed against the life of Bokassa from beginning to end. Upon achieving the presidency of the Central African Republic he was able to more fruitfully follow this obsession, an obsession that would take him deep into notoriety in a forlorn and costly quest to emulate the achievements of the Little Corporal.

Bonaparte was born on the Mediterranean island of Corsica, an offshore *région* of France, to a family of modest local standing.

Charles de Gaulle.
Source: Wikicommons

Georges Pompidou.
Source: Wikicommons

Mobuto Sese Seko
Source: Wikicommons

Valéry Giscard d'Estaing
Source: Wikicommons

He entered the French army and rose through the ranks steadily, first achieving great military stature, then acquiring considerable political influence. In due course he reinstated the French Empire and crowned himself emperor. He was a man characterized by military brilliance, enormous ambition and a desire for absolute power.

Bokassa was deeply enthralled by the symbolism of this, and what it might mean for him. That a social outsider could enter, rise to the pinnacle of, and dominate a nation such as France, by dint of both divine destiny and an unassailable personal capacity, fed very much into the self-image that Bokassa had long entertained. Within the unfettered and permissive environment of black African politics, where the Machiavellian practice was raw, unmodified and undisguised, such outrageous ambition was quite plausible.

In the aftermath of the coup, many observing from the outside, and particularly those in France, were left with the impression that the whole affair had been rather bloodless bearing in mind the standards of the times. Some killing had taken place, and Bokassa had attended early to the business of cleaning house but, once the dust had settled, an initial disdain on the part of the French warmed somewhat. Bokassa revealed himself as a passionate Francophile and a man of such obvious venality that the usual devices of corruption would render him infinitely reliable.

De Gaulle himself, although ambivalent to his ascension, had a low personal regard for Bokassa and wasted very little time dealing with him. A more sympathetic link with the *métropole* was offered by Jacques Foccart, chief of staff for African affairs under both Charles de Gaulle and Georges Pompidou, and the principal architect of *Françafrique*, France's post independence relationship with its erstwhile colonies.

La Foque, as he was better known, was in charge of African affairs from 1960 to 1974, and negotiated all the most important French-African political issues at the time, as well as directing the African activities of the SDECE (*Service de Documentation Extérieur et de Contre-Espionnage*), the French external intelligence agency. He was very close to most African leaders, from whom he acquired a steady stream of information, supplemented by gossip selected from the small cells of African intellectuals, opposition figures and activists whom he spent many years cultivating, information which was seldom if ever shared directly with the Ministry of Foreign Affairs in Paris, or with any of its embassies in Africa. He in fact played such an important role in French–African policy that, after de Gaulle, he was often regarded as the most influential man of the Fifth Republic.

Foccart was known for his 'network', and in fact the 'Foccart Network' is almost a modern euphemism for the kind of multi–layered, and often contradictory friendships, alliances and relationships that an intelligence man must develop to function effectively within the dark and soft underbelly of an environment like Africa. That this involved duplicity, double standards, betrayal when necessary, and an ability to ignore some of the more obvious and odious shortfalls of governance in Cold War Africa goes without saying. Some of Foccart's closest relationships were with political actors such as Bokassa himself, Mobuto Sese Seko and Omar Bongo, who represented the worst of black African governance, but also dealings on the opposite side of the spectrum, with South Africa, Rhodesia and colonial Mozambique and Angola.

An insight on the methods Foccart applied in the subterranean commerce he maintained with his network of African plutocrats is given by the head of SDECE from 1970 to 1981, Count Alexandre de Marenches, in his personal memoir, *The Evil Empire*:

> Foccart was the General's [de Gaulle] man for special, or so called 'reserved' affairs. He had built up a number of networks, in black Africa especially, and unfortunately their precise nature became confused. There were official networks and unofficial networks. This whole period in the history of the French Secret Service was compromised and marred by the proliferation of individuals who at the time and thereafter came to be known as *barbouzes*, unofficial secret agents (literally, 'wearing false beards'). One of the assignments entrusted to me by President Pompidou was to put an end to the operations undertaken by these *barbouzes*, who were impossible to handle and beyond control. In secret service there needs to be and impeccable code of conduct and extremely strict discipline. There is a strong temptation for people to make money—to trade information and secrets for

financial gain. There is no doubt at all that the presence of *barbouzes* in different African states encouraged those in question to become businessmen, traders, which it was not for them to be.[9]

Foccart certainly did have a unique style. An unassuming, bespectacled and balding man, when word seeped out through the networks that he was on his way, or had been seen here or there in Africa, the press and security services across the continent would be alerted to the fact that something was afoot. However, it was through his role as de Gaulle's personal agent and fix-it man in Africa that the special, personalized style of Francophone relations evolved. His Machiavellian approach was visible in many a coup and manipulation in French-speaking Africa over the years. He served most effectively under de Gaulle, but was retained under Georges Pompidou and, to a lesser extent, under President Valéry Giscard d'Estaing, under whose rule a final denouement with Bokassa would be enacted.

To all three French Presidents, Jean-Bédel Bokassa represented an enigma. Fawningly desirous of recognition, he cultivated the myth that he and de Gaulle were fast friends and confederates; he having served under the great general during the dark days of Vichy, service for which he suggested de Gaulle gave personal recognition. De Gaulle, of course, in his particularly unforgiving manner, allowed the ice to break sufficiently to only once refer to Bokassa as a "good bloke". For the most part he saw the Central African demagogue for what he was, and responded to him strictly according to the requirements of his current foreign policy, and nothing more. The same was true for Pompidou. Both men were happy to leave the matter of French policy in the Central African Republic to Foccart, and if Marenches was even partially accurate in his assessment of Foccart's African political networks, Foccart was very much the kind of Frenchman that an African like Bokassa could understand.

Foccart adopted a hear-no-evil, see-no-evil attitude to Bokassa, ignoring his mood swings, his wildly irrational style of government and the clear evidence of his mental imbalance. Within the strategic region of Central Africa, Chad was perhaps the more important pawn in the game than the Central African Republic, which in fact served French interests primarily as a rear base for operations in Chad, and little more. France maintained numerous military agreements with friendly African governments within its sphere of influence, with the objective of securing French involvement and influence in the region and ensuring the survival of compliant and friendly African leaders.

Bokassa, in the meanwhile, was not remiss in laying the usual foundations of his rule. In 1972 he established himself as president for life, adopting the military rank of marshal as reward for supreme services to the state. Despite this disturbing preoccupation with personal embellishment, there seemed at first to be a feeling that Bokassa had arrived in office with a sense of mission to reform the government, and for a while he actively grandstanded that illusion. Very quickly, however, the

mask began to slip. Economic malfeasance was, of course, his first visible concession to the necessity of political patronage, and while Bokassa himself made free with the resources of state and the national treasury, he grumbled periodically about the general level of corruption in his government, and made known whenever necessary his determination to clean up his administration. Quite as he was uttering these high-sounding proclamations he was also busily acquiring a string of valuable properties in Europe, among which were four châteaux in France, a fifty-room Paris mansion, houses in Nice and Toulouse and a villa in Berne. At home he ordered an enormous 'ancestral home' to be constructed outside the hamlet of Berengo, fifty miles from Bangui, to which was commissioned motorway access from the capital. This presidential estate contained private houses, a range of lavish apartments for foreign dignitaries, all extensively decorated with fine art, gilt mirrors and reproduction and actual antique furniture of the most lavish and ostentatious imperial styling.

As all this was underway he continued to promote morality, austerity, honesty and hard work as the new catchphrases of public life. All the disappointments of independence, he decreed, fermented by the weak and vacillating Dacko, would now be reversed, and Boganda's dream for the republic would at last be realized. A cult of personality, meanwhile, began to emerge, with omnipresent portraiture, speechifying and public imagery that pervaded every aspect of life. The naming of buildings, institutions and boulevards after himself soon followed, with the first hints of even greater ambition yet emerging with carefully placed but apparently off-hand comments during many of his extensive foreign junkets that he, Bokassa, considered himself to be an "absolute monarch".[10]

Much of the financial and military support for all of this was provided by the French, anxious against a backdrop of military intervention in Chad, and the persistent territorial ambitions of Libya's eccentric, but virulently revolutionary Colonel Gadaffi, to ensure that the Central African Republic remained firmly within the French sphere of influence. The excesses of Bokassa's rule had not at that point begun to eclipse those of others, such as Mobuto Sese Seko of Zaire, a French favourite, or Equatorial Guinea's farcical Francisco Macías Nguema. Occasional tendencies for Bokassa to indicate an ideological tilt eastward were apt to be aimed at spurring the French towards yet greater economic support, a gambit that usually succeeded, albeit reluctantly, and with considerable irritation on the part of presidents with no personal affinity toward Bokassa whatsoever.

This low-level antipathy was eased somewhat in 1974 when the French presidency passed to the flamboyant, vain and rather disingenuous Valéry Giscard d'Estaing. The two met at the 1970 funeral of Charles de Gaulle, at a time when Giscard was serving as finance minister. Here was a man somewhat more influenced by personal pleasures than Pompidou had been, and certainly de Gaulle, and an apparently warm relationship was kindled between him and Bokassa. This allowed the French president to indulge in, among other things, a passion for hunting. Bokassa placed at his

Forces Armées Centrafricaines. Source: Wikicommons

A young Colonel Gaddafi.
Source: Wikicommons

Macias Nguema.
Source: Wikicommons

disposal the resources of the Zemongo Faunal Reserve, situated in the southeast of the republic and measuring some two million hectares; here Giscard was reputed to have personally killed fifty elephants and countless other wild animals, including rhinoceros.

Giscard claimed to have descended from the Bourbons via an illegitimate branch on his mother's side. He placed a great deal of store in this, and such august pretensions could have done little to dampen Bokassa's own imperial aspirations. Where Bokassa had been dismissed outright by de Gaulle and Pompidou as a buffoon, and a disappointing by-product of an over-hasty granting of independence to the colonies, Giscard was friendlier, more approachable, and perhaps even a little corruptible. The 'special relationship' that de Gaulle and Pompidou had delegated somewhat to Foccart was taken up with interest by Giscard himself, and in fact his first state visit as president was taken to the Central African Republic. Here he was introduced to the big-game hunting potential of the territory; the fact that, as a personal friend of the president, he enjoyed unrestricted use of arguably one of the last great undisturbed wilderness regions of Africa.

On 4 December 1976, meanwhile, Bokassa set in motion one of the greatest follies of African extravagance in a period of outrageous political theatre. At a congress of the country's single party it was announced by the president that henceforth the Central African Republic would be known as the Central African Empire, and that his coronation as emperor would take place a year from that date, the date, incidentally, upon which Napoleon had himself been coronated.

With neither consultation nor dialogue, the constitution of the republic was altered to accommodate this change of status, and with the briefest of pauses to establish the reaction of the world, Bokassa gleefully plunged into the organization of an event that would mark the nadir of black Africa's first independent political generation. The task of organizing the spectacle was given to Bokassa's Prime Minister, Ange-Félix Patassé, who undertook it with patriotic zeal. While the world looked on, this 'tropical farce' went ahead against a barrage of press ridicule, but with the

apparent collusion, and indeed enthusiastic support, of the French. Indeed, it was from France that all the trappings of monarchy were ordered: an imperial crown, a golden throne in the shape of an eagle and an antique coach complete with thoroughbred horses, coronation robes, brass helmets and breastplates for the Imperial Guard and some sixty Mercedes Benz limousines for the conveyance of the anticipated 5000 guests.

The coronation took place on 4 December 1977 at the Palais des Sports Jean-Bédel Bokassa, on Bokassa Avenue, alongside the Université Jean-Bédel Bokassa in the presence of an impressive gathering of dignitaries. Among thesde, to the Emperor's disappointment, included no heads of state or fellow monarchs, nor the Pope who Bokassa lobbied relentlessly to perform the ceremony, nor, indeed, Giscard himself, who thought better of it.

The $20 million price tag in an insolvent and deeply poor nation was met with international press condemnation. The French put on a brave face, with Cooperation Minister Robert Galley venturing to comment that criticism of such a spectacle in Africa when it was commonplace in Europe smacked of racism. Giscard d'Estaing, meanwhile, quietly let it be known that Paris would arrange compensation for all unpaid expenses. As the emperor himself once put it, "Everything here was financed by the French government. We ask the French for money, get it and waste it."[11]

And such might have remained the case but for Bokassa himself. As time progressed the emperor grew progressively less tethered to reality and increasingly unrestrained in his behaviour. There was an initial period of circumspection both regionally and internationally with regards Bokassa's grand delusion, but in due course he received the international recognition he desired, whereupon he determined to enjoy his wealth, power and status to the maximum.

Bokassa's principal error was perhaps, during a lean period, to convert to Islam and court the favour of the Gadaffi regime in Libya for economic grants and support. Gadaffi's interest in the Central African Empire lay mainly in the military air base of Bouar in furtherance of his own military and territorial ambitions. Marenches makes mention of this in his book *The Evil Empire*:

The strategy which Colonel Gaddafi, the Libyan leader, had in mind was to occupy Chad and then the Central

African Republic, just below it. Once there, he would have found himself on a commanding site, not unlike the Plateau of Pratzen which enabled Napoleon to establish his strategy for the Battle of Austerliz in 1805.[12]

Gaddafi was then five years or so into his chairmanship of the Revolutionary Command Council of Libya. He was blessed with considerable acumen and a great deal of oil revenue, and had various interests in Africa, not least a regional or continental union. Here he saw a place for himself astride the continent that was not unlike Bokassa's own grandiose self-image. Gadaffi in fact represented a fifth column of threat in Africa during the Cold War era, and although he was, on the whole, more closely aligned to the east, his pleasure was the support of anarchic, nationalist terror groups and forming visible associations with some of the most maligned of global leaders.

Bokassa's second cardinal error was to become too deeply imbibed with the myth of his own destiny, and too comfortable in the unassailability of his own position. His propensity for violence began to intrude on the fairytale very soon after his coronation. The brutality of the Bokassa regime prior to this had not borne particular comparison to others active on the African stage at that time, and with the comic tragedy of Idi Amin swiftly moving to its climax, Bokassa would have needed to lose himself in absolute lunacy in order for his crimes to be noticed. In due course, however, this was precisely what he did.

The dominoes of Bokassa's collapse began to fall on 19 January 1978 with the start of a series of student protests over an edict that all pupils in the country buy and wear exclusively new school uniforms manufactured by a textile factory, and sold through a retail chain that were both owned by the Bokassa family. The demonstrations were joined by the urban unemployed and destitute, of which there were many, and quickly degenerated into riots. These were brutally repressed by the Imperial Guard as Bokassa did not wholly trust the army. However, student, teacher and civil servant demonstrations continued regardless.

In April Bokassa ordered that scores of students be rounded up and taken to the notorious Ngaragba prison. In one instance some thirty students were forced into a cell designed for one, and in another twenty, with the doors then jammed shut and the suffocating knot left until the following day. When the doors were opened again it was revealed that many had died. Further reports stated that Bokassa himself had visited the prison and added his arm to the beatings that were delivered throughout the night.

This was, of course, vehemently denied by Bokassa but, despite his intense lobbying to suppress the findings, an independent judicial inquiry later concluded: "In the month of April 1979 the massacre of about one hundred children was carried out under the orders of Emperor Bokassa and almost certainly with his personal participation."[13] In France he was dubbed by the press the 'Butcher of Bangui'. The French up until that point had put up with much. Aid had flowed consistently, with just an occasional ebb here. Bokassa had been permitted to make free with such iconic French names as Napoleon and de Gaulle, had been accepted at the Élysée Palace as legitimate, if not authentic, and indeed Giscard had allowed himself to be compromised by hunting concessions, lavish imperial hospitality and even grandiose gifts of diamonds, but the student massacre proved a step too far. After a great deal of prevarication and soul searching, the decision to bring Bokassa down was taken, and thereafter it was simply a matter of time.

CHAPTER THREE:
OPERATION *BARRACUDA*

"When you want to kill your dog, accuse it of having rabies"
—Bokassa

The findings of the independent judicial inquiry conducted into the Bangui massacre were published at an extremely sensitive time for French President Valéry Giscard d'Estaing. His political opponent, François Mitterrand, a left-leaning political brawler, seized on Giscard's rather ill-advised relationship with the now utterly discredited 'Butcher of Bangui', and with it began drawing public attention to the *l'affaire des diamants*, the so called Diamond Affair, that had recently been exposed by French satirical newspaper, *Le Canard Enchaîné*. The gifts of diamonds that Giscard had apparently accepted indebted him to Bokassa, and if not that, then at very least it revealed a far too cosy relationship between the head of a G7 state and a bloodstained affiliate of the lunatic fringe of African politics.

Giscard's response was to admit that he had received diamonds but these he dismissed as gems of little value, after which he refused to dignify with a reply any accusations that he said were based on forged documents. This reply of offended dignity cut very little ice and the president's standing was damaged as a consequence.

Thus it became imperative for Giscard to launch some sort of discernable action to right the balance of French complicity in events in Bangui. It had also become clear that Bokassa would never relinquish power voluntarily. France could, with some ease, have tightened the economic noose sufficiently to strangle the regime, but with that would have come the danger of Bokassa turning to Libya once again, and this, under the political conditions of the time, represented an unacceptable risk. Incautious French military intervention in the country carried similar risks, both practical and political. The matter had to be considered very carefully, and for this Giscard turned to Alexandre de Marenches, head of the

François Mitterand, 1984.
Source: Wikicommons

Alexandre de Marenches.
Source: Wikicommons

Libyan president, Colonel Gadaffi.
Source: Wikicommons

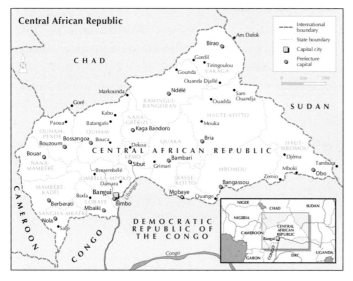

Service de Documentation Extérieure et de Contre-Espionnage, or the SDECE, France's external intelligence agency.

De Marenches presents his own factually lean, but colourful, account of events that followed in his memoir, *The Evil Empire*. In it he states that the trigger for action was not Giscard's embarrassment or the electoral uncertainties caused by *l'affaire des diamants*, but the question of forestalling Libyan influence in the region: "The truth is that what the country [Central African Empire] does provide us good conditions in which to hunt big game. And why indeed should the practice of this sport be incompatible with the governance of France?"[14]

Why indeed. De Marenches claimed to have received intelligence reports indicating the arrival in the Central African Empire of elements of Libyan Special Forces. This, he concluded, could quite easily have been the precursor to the appearance in the territory of Cubans, or, indeed Soviets or East Germans. The situation, he stated, was urgent, and needed to be dealt with immediately. A civil war in Chad that had strong religious overtones was compromising the French position in the country and adding leverage to an already deeply interested Gaddafi. In 1978 the first substantive French intervention in Chad in support of the government took place.[2] As de Marenches saw it: "The

---

[2] Further reading: *Africa's Thirty Years War: Libya, Chad, and the Sudan, 1963–1993.* J. Millard Burr & Robert O. Collins. (Westview Press. Boulder, CO. 1999)

matter of Chad and the Central African Republic was then held to be of high strategic importance, not just for France but for the defence of our black African family. To avoid having a full-scale war on our hands, action had to be taken swiftly, surgery applied. The moment had come to get rid of poor old Bokassa."[15]

Getting rid of 'poor old' Bokassa was likely to be the easiest part of the operation. Ensuring his replacement with a successor friendly to French interests would prove a little more tricky. This could not be left to chance and certainly it could not be left to caprices of democratic determination. A replacement for Bokassa would need to be carefully chosen, although unfortunately, upon examination of the possible candidates, all were found wanting.

It so happened that David Dacko was at that time living in exile in Paris. Dacko, however, was in poor health and oppressed by a morbid fear of Bokassa. He was initially extremely reluctant to entertain any suggestion of a return to Bangui and a resumption of the office that had been wrested from him so abruptly a decade earlier. He was visited several times at his Paris apartment by de Marenches who, with a combination of flattery and appeal, succeeded in weakening his resolve.

When finally Dacko agreed, he was moved into an apartment on the Rue de Berri, just off the Champs Élysées. It was necessary that he be ready to leave France at a moment's notice as detailed arrangements were being put in place. Against the risk that he might change his mind he was placed under twenty-four-hour surveillance. In the meanwhile, the French government consulted with the principal heads of state in the region—notably Omar Bongo of Gabon, Houphouët-Boigny of Côte d'Ivoire, Mobutu Sese Seko of Zaire and Senghor of Senegal—all of whom gave their approval to the French plan.

The details of the plan were simple. All aid to Bangui, with the exception of humanitarian projects, was to be cut off, which was intended to put pressure on Bokassa as well as give some sense to the French media that Giscard was dealing firmly with the tyrant. A military operation would follow, but this was to be put into effect only when Bokassa was out of the country, the rationale here being the belief that Bokassa's imperial guard would be less inclined to fight if he himself was absent. The military operation was codenamed Opération *Barracuda*; a big fish consuming a little fish

Insignia of the 3rd Régiment Parachutiste d'Infanterie de Marine. *Source: Wikicommons*

Lt.-Col Marcel 'Bruno' Bigeard. *Source: Wikicommons*

Bizerte, 1961. *Source: Wikicommons*

Insignia of the 8th Régiment Parachutiste d'Infanterie de Marine. *Source: Wikicommons*

Insignia of the 1st Régiment Parachutiste d'Infanterie de Marine. *Source: Wikicommons*

was no doubt the intended symbolism here. No significant opposition was anticipated on the ground, but the surgical nature of the intended strike required detailed planning based on current and accurate intelligence. The main strike force was to consist of two elite French units poised within a short flying distance of Bangui, and a third deployed from the metropole.

The first of the regionally based units was a 200-man company of the 3rd Régiment Parachutiste d'Infanterie de Marine, or RPIMa. Between 12 and 17 September, 1979, these men had been deployed on joint military manoeuvres in Zaire's Shaba Province with elements of Mobuto's army. At the conclusion of this exercise the unit was flown back to its base in Libreville, Gabon, where the men had scarcely settled back in when the alert was received. The second strike force would comprise two companies, some 400 men, of the 8th Régiment Parachutiste d'Infanterie de Marine, the famous Red Berets, which at that time was stationed in N'Djaména, the Chadian capital, among the 2,500 or so French troops supporting the government of President Goukouni Oueddei.

Both these were elite French units and both were part of the 11th Parachute Brigade headquartered in Balma on the outskirts of Toulouse. The older of the two units was the 3rd. It had been formed initially in January 1948 as the 3rd Colonial Commando Parachute Battalion and deployed to French Indochina in October of the same year. It was twice cited in the order of battle before being disbanded after suffering considerable loss at That Khe. It was reformed in December 1951 and renamed in May the following year the 3rd Colonial Parachute Battalion. It once again

achieved distinction in Indochina. Dissolved again in 1953, it provided a framework for the 5th Vietnamese Parachute Battalion. It was finally reformed in June 1955 as the 3rd Colonial Parachute Regiment under the command of one of France's most decorated soldiers, Lieutenant-Colonel Marcel 'Bruno' Bigeard, of Dien Bien Phu fame and widely regarded as the father of French 'unconventional' warfare. As part of the 10th Parachute Division, the unit was active in all the major operations in Algeria, including in combat around Bizerte. It was renamed 3rd Marine Infantry Parachute Regiment in December 1958. In July 1962 the regiment was classified as a fully regular unit.

The 8th was created in February 1951 as the 8th Colonial Parachute Battalion, forming part of the greater French union forces. It saw action at Lai-Chau, Hoa Binh, Langson and during the epic disaster of Dien Bien Phu. It was mentioned in dispatches four times for valour, but was dissolved on 19 May 1954 after Dien Bien Phu. In May 1956, the unit was recreated as the 8th Colonial Parachute Regiment, participating in operations against the Algerian National Liberation Front (FLN), most notably at El Kiffene, Ain El Kesseub and Tarf. In 1961 the regiment relocated to Nancy in the northeast of France to form part of the 11th Light Division. Two years later the regimental headquarters moved to Castres, east of Toulouse.

Launching from the French mainland, and accompanying the handpicked presidential replacement, would be a small detachment of 130 men of the 1st Régiment Parachutiste d'Infanterie de Marine, commanded by Brigadier-General Jacques Guichard. These were the elite troops—an associate corps of the British SAS and arguably the most august unit in the French special force formation—that would make up the first boots on the ground in Bangui.

The 1er RPIMa was, and remains, one of the most highly pedigreed units in the French special forces stable. The origins of the unit date back to the Second World War when it was formed as *1ère Compagnie d'Infanterie de l'Air* in Britain, re-designated *1ère Compagnie de Chasseurs Parachutistes* (1e CCP) under legendary Free French Captain Georges Bergé, recognized at that time on both sides of the Channel as a daring commando tactician and operative. The unit consisted of some fifty French paratroopers

Puma helicopter at M'poko airbase displaying a 20mm canon.

who were seconded to the Special Air Service during the North Africa campaign, contributing to many successful operations in Africa, Crete, France, Belgium, Holland and Germany. The 1er RPIMa still retains the iconic dagger insignia symbol and the motto *Qui Ose Gagne*, or Who Dares Wins.

The regiment is a derivative of the two Free French Special Air Service (SAS) units: 3 SAS (3e RCP) and 4 SAS (2e RCP). On 1 October 1945, 3 and 4 SAS were handed over to the French army. The regiment was restructured after returning from Indochina after which it acted as training depot for the colonial parachute force during the Algerian war. It continued in this function until 1974 when it became a special forces regiment.

This was a great deal of force to be throwing at the anaemic armed forces of the Central African Empire, so clearly de Marenches and others on the planning committee had resolved to take no chances. The assault, if it was to be such, was to take the form of an airborne landing at Bangui's M'poko international airport, from where units would spread out to seize key installations in the city. Bangui, by international standards, was not a large urban centre, and it was anticipated that what risk to the success of the operation there might be would come from the Presidential, or Imperial Guard, a force numbering some 1,000 men possessing slightly higher training and equipment than the regular forces of the territory. In the past, the latter had in fact tended to have been kept unarmed due to the customary distrust a dictator such as Bokassa might feel toward the very vehicle that had brought him to power.

Ground intelligence, meanwhile, was excellent, and drawn from a variety of civilian, diplomatic and intelligence sources. M'poko international airport was protected by a guard detachment supported by two machine-gun posts. The French were careful to ascertain which tribe made up a majority of the garrison, in order that a member of the strike force who was conversant in the necessary dialect was present. It was also known that the army had

not been paid for several months and that with rampant inflation the local currency was largely worthless anyway. The landing would be supported by a handful of local and international currencies that those on the ground shrewdly suggested would be more potent in a pinch than any amount of military hardware.

In the meanwhile Bokassa played neatly into the hands of the plotters by leaving the country after fretting anxiously about the economic squeeze and headed to Tripoli where he hoped, as had been anticipated by the French, to rekindle a relationship with the Libyan leader, Colonel Gaddaffi.

At 08:30 on Wednesday, 19 September, the imperial Caravelle [a gift from France] took off from Berengo carrying Bokassa and his delegation. This information was immediately communicated to Paris by none other than Henri Maïdou, Bokassa's prime minister. A secondary, but no less valuable source of intelligence, was French ambassador, Robert Picquet, and his associate, military attaché, Colonel Mazza.

At 09:30 the following morning, a grey Citroën sedan came to a halt opposite David Dacko's Paris apartment. An SDECE agent stepped out of the car and entered the building to collect the president-in-waiting who had been cooling his heels for a week in a state of nervous anxiety. He was escorted to a nearby airfield from where he was flown to the town of Tarbes on the northern slopes of the Pyrenees. There, parked on the runway, stood two C-160 Transall long-distance military transport aircraft. Seated within were the 130 men of the 1st Régiment Parachutiste d'Infanterie de Marine, commanded by Brigadier-General Jacques Guichard.

The sudden reality of all this shocked an apprehensive Dacko as he entered the aircraft, at which point his nerve failed him. By then, however, it was too late. His appeals to be let off the aircraft were ignored, and as one followed the other into the cool evening sky, and settled on a southeasterly flight path across the Mediterranean, he was ordered into a seat in a corner of the cockpit where he sat apart from the troops, and deep within his own thoughts.

Bokassa, in the meanwhile, had arrived in Tripoli to be greeted by a government official and told that Gadaffi had been detained and would meet him the following day in Benghazi. That meeting was also delayed sufficiently for Bokassa to be left in no doubt that negotiations with Gaddafi would be conducted on the latter's terms. Gaddafi's interest in Central Africa was strategic. He wanted control of the military base at Bouar, in exchange for which, through the Libyan Embassy in Bangui, he undertook to pay military and civil-services wages, as well as outstanding student bursaries. Although somewhat piqued at the working reception he had received, accustomed as he was to the lavish pomp and ceremony customary for a monarch, Bokassa was

Soldiers of the 8th RPIMa in position in Bangui.
Source: Ministère de la Défense

delighted with the result he had achieved, and retired to his hotel in Benghazi in fine humour. By then, after a brief refuelling stop in N'Djamena, the French had already landed in Bangui. Intelligence had indicated the precise time that the airport would close for the night, although, on this particular evening, it appeared that the control tower was to remain open to receive an Egyptian aircraft that had developed problems and would be arriving late. De Marenches states, rather enigmatically, that, from his control centre in Paris, he was able "by a stroke of fortune—partly luck and partly deftness—[we managed] in the course of the next few hours to make it develop engine failure."[16]

Two French SDECE *barbouzes* were by then waiting in the shadows on the tarmac of M'poko international airport and as the two aircraft touched down, they were guided onto the apron by flashlight. Thereafter things moved quickly. Since the Egyptian aircraft had been delayed the airport was locked up and the staff largely absent. Dacko and his vehicle were in the second Transall and there he waited, apparently with his wife, until the airport was secured.

The assault group made its way quickly toward the building where a nervous guard detachment, having observed events and concluded accurately that something was amiss, had taken refuge with sub-machine guns poised at the doors and windows. The officer who was conversant in the appropriate indigenous dialect stood a short distance away and addressed the men inside through a loudspeaker: "We have come here not with any territorial claim on you," he began, "but simply to allow your country to rid itself of a tyrant, and if possible to bring back democratic government."

There followed a momentary pause as this news was digested. Then, with calm military efficacy, it was added: "We know that you have not been paid for three months. Kindly form a queue along the wall."[17]

With that a table and chair was set down and a paymaster took his seat, opened a record book, opened a box filled with cash and waited patiently as this extraordinary turn of events was fully absorbed by the nervous black troops. When it was ascertained that

all was in order and this was not a trap, each man put down his gun, broke into a broad smile and formed a queue as instructed for payment in hard currency. Officers were permitted to retain their weapons but the other ranks were ordered to stack them to one side. There were none who objected.

Thus, and without a shot being fired, the airport was secure. From there, with local officers as guides, French troops in armoured cars fanned out to occupy strategic points within the city. David Dacko remained at the airport until it was confirmed that Bangui was in French hands, after which he was driven under armed escort to the local radio station, where, at 11:00 local time, he made the following announcement:

This is David Dacko speaking . . . The regime of Bokassa I has disintegrated. Its final act was the massacre of a hundred children bringing universal condemnation and ultimately bringing the regime down. For fourteen years the country has been exploited by the man who proclaimed himself emperor and dragged our image in the mud by his excesses and delusions of grandeur.[18]

As Dacko was making this proclamation, support troops of the of the 3rd and 8th *Régiment Parachutiste d'Infanterie de Marine* were coming in to land at M'poko international airport. The invasion force, however, had met no resistance whatsoever. Local troops threw down their weapons the moment that the news became general. The Imperial Guard stationed at the Imperial Palace at Berengo, remained at their posts for a few hours, but ultimately chose to abandon their arms and uniforms and disappear in preference to a shootout with the French. The Central African Empire was no more.

The news was broken to Bokassa that morning by the Libyan ambassador, Ali Treiki, who interrupted the first unbroken sleep that the emperor had enjoyed since the publication of the judicial inquiry. Initially there was some doubt that the information circulating was accurate, but before too long the melancholy truth was confirmed, and Bokassa sat watching the sunrise over the city of Benghazi in a deep depression. He appealed to Gaddafi, but was informed that the Libyan leader had left, no doubt having heard the news himself and read the situation for what it was. Bokassa was on his own.

No effort was made by the Libyans to interfere with Bokassa's departure. The Caravelle jet left Benghazi and after a brief stop for refuelling in Tripoli, it took off northward in the direction of Paris. For the French news of this created a rather sensitive conundrum. Having ousted Bokassa the question now became what to do with him. First at Orly, and then Roissy, permission to land was denied. It was not until Bokassa threatened to land on a highway that permission was granted for the aircraft to touch down at Evreux military base, west of Paris. However, upon landing, no disembarkation was permitted. A long hiatus ensued. Bokassa was a French citizen and could not easily be denied entry, but demonstrators heckling Bokassa were already gathering outside the airport. Temporary asylum was eventually granted the ex-emperor by Félix Houphouët-Boigny of Côte d'Ivoire.

Thus, as Bokassa's aircraft was turned around and directed south again, his vast assets in the Central African Republic were being redistributed. Much of what he owned found its way into the hands of Dacko and others of his regime, while the accoutrements of power—his crown along with other items of ceremonial importance and value—were sequestered by French troops and removed from the country. These, it might be supposed, remain in France under the care of the Secret Service. It was widely reported that Bokassa's personal archive was located and removed by French forces against the risk that further embarrassment be caused Giscard if too many details of his relationship with Bokassa should come to light.

CHAPTER FOUR:
THE FRENCH MILITARY IN AFRICA

"By establishing France in Africa we shall guarantee
the peace of Europe"
—Charles Maurice de Talleyrand
on Napoleon's Egyptian expedition, 1798

It would not be entirely true to say that the Diamond Affair cost Valéry Giscard d'Estaing his presidency, but it added much to a general perception of sleaze that accompanied a rather haughty and disparaging leadership. And neither did the matter end once Bokassa had been deposed. The French political opposition was quick to press home its advantage. Mitterrand condemned Giscard's personal junkets to the territory in lavish terms, highlighting the big-game hunting, and of course, the undeclared personal gifts of ivory and diamonds.

Giscard responded with predictable bombast and indignation, which more than anything else, painted a picture of a man in a tight corner. The October 1979 headline of the much-hated satirical monthly, *Canard Enchaîné*, proclaimed with glee: "When Giscard was pocketing Bokassa's diamonds ..."

The fact of these gifts having been made was confirmed indirectly by the Élysée Palace when the value of the gifts, estimated by the press to be upward of $250,000, was disputed. François Mitterrand, of course, seized the opportunity and immediately renewed demands for a parliamentary investigation into the degree of Giscard's personal involvement with Bokassa, and indeed that of other high-ranking French officials similarly tainted with corruption.

Soon after, and to add to Giscard's discomfiture, the transcript of a document dated March 1973 surfaced, signed by Bokassa, that purported to request the local *comptoir national du diamante* to arrange a *plaquette* of diamonds, some 30 carats in all, as a personal gift from the emperor to Giscard, at that time serving as finance minister. *Canard Enchaîné* went further, alleging that Bokassa had made a regular habit of this sort of thing, showering Giscard with a variety of expensive gifts during the latter's frequent visits to Centrafrique, none of which was ever refused, or declared, as required by French law.

The whole business was purported to have begun as early as 1967, when elephant tusks and ivory carvings were given to Giscard to accompany his frequent hunting expeditions, after which diamonds tended to be the gift befitting a president. The distribution of this sort of largesse was not confined to Giscard either, but apparently extended to his brother Olivier and his two cousins Jacques and François. Other beneficiaries named included Robert Galley, René Journiac, and the Minister of Defence, Yvon Bourges. The *Canard Enchaîné* went on to claim that the 'Barracudas' had seized the archives at Bokassa's palace at Berengo precisely because they contained sensitive documents pertaining to the Giscard administration's relations with the Central African Empire.

Thereafter the local and international press enjoyed a jamboree of negative reportage against Giscard, adding nothing to the weight of his presidential campaign and bringing into question his integrity with ever more lurid and penetrating reports. This in many ways obscured the fact that much Franco–African entente from the period of the Free French to date had been undertaken, and indeed had been successful as a consequence of, the sort of personal relationships wherein this sort of thing might be expected to happen. Pompidou had enjoyed a personal friendship of long standing with Léopold Senghor, and had Senghor been a victim of the kind of public displays that Bokassa so loved, it is possible that Pompidou too might have suffered similar negative exposure.

Giscard's style of management and his Africa policy were in fact very successful, and when examined across the spectrum of economic, cultural and military development, it can be seen that he did much, particularly from the middle of his term of office onward, to strengthen the French military role in Africa, and in general to bolster the notion of Franco–African unity. Each French president, from Charles de Gaulle on, has in one way or another recognized and acted upon the importance of the French–

An illustration of the French occupation of Egypt.
Source: Wikicommons

African relationship, particularly in military terms, a relationship that has a surprisingly long history.

The history of French military involvement in Africa can in fact be traced back as far as the French occupation of Egypt that took place during the Napoleonic period between 1798 and 1801. Although this was separated by almost a century from the massive occupation of the continent that occurred during the closing decades of the 19th century, it had about it all the same elements. A bold, and some would say rash, global-strategic manoeuvre was justified, and again, some would say, adulterated, by a high-minded desire to bring enlightenment to the Orient, and moreover to rescue the indolent native from himself.

In fact the expedition was more adroitly defined by the brilliant but impetuous Napoleon Bonaparte as a grand manoeuvre to isolate Britain from India, as a precursor to a more substantive engagement, and perhaps even an opportunity for Napoleon to stage a grand march in the Alexandrian style to the banks of the Ganges. "I was full of dreams," Napoleon said of this objective: "I saw myself founding a new religion, marching into Asia riding an elephant, a turban on my head, and in my hand the new Koran."[19] From the point of view of the Directory Government in Paris it was an opportunity to remove this overly ambitious Corsican from the mainland and preoccupy him with some aspiration other than absolute power.

However, if this was to be the blueprint of later European imperial adventure, then it was a reasonably accurate one. A huge expeditionary force by the standards of the times was assembled on the French Mediterranean coast, accompanied by a cohort of some 160 scholars, who would later form the Institut d'Égypte. Along with them travelled a library of 215,000 books and a printing press with type appropriate for both western and oriental languages, all obtained from the Vatican stores and library. Here was an undertaking based on the notion of conquest, and retention of power, through intellectual and administrative authority as much as military. The *Description de l'Égypte*, a huge multi-volume collection, compiled by the scholars of the Institut d'Égypte upon the order of Napoleon, later became the principal resource for documenting and commemorating the French expedition to the Near East, and was used by travellers, generals and scholars for similar ends deep into the succeeding century.

Admiral Horatio Nelson. *Source: Wikicommons*

The expedition duly embarked and was crowned by early military success. Malta was seized for France en route, after which the French successfully evaded the British fleet under Admiral Horatio Nelson, landing east of Alexandria on 1 June 1798. The famous port city, although fortified, fell to the French with a minimum of resistance, after which Napoleon's troops marched on to conquer the whole of Upper Egypt.

Egypt was formally a province of the Ottoman Empire, but was substantively governed by the Mamelukes, an unusual configuration of slave warriors that evolved under the tutelage of the Ottomans to become the backbone of their military forces. Known also as *ghulams*, or pages, most were purchased in the Caucuses as children, after which they were subjected to rigorous training and discipline, which in due course gave rise to a supremely professional and politically ambivalent military caste. As was inevitable, some among the Mameluks grew to be extremely powerful, and in 1260 the Mameluke Baybars seized the throne of Egypt, beginning a pattern of rule by monarchs of slave-soldier origin, arguably the most culturally and economically successful period in the history of medieval Egypt.

Needless to say the French saw the Mamelukes as less than a ruling caste of unique refinement and more a hierarchy of robber barons soaked in blood and steeped in violence, which certainly was some part of their myth. Whatever might have been the truth, Mameluke rule of Egypt effectively ended on 21 July 1798, when an army of some 50,000 Mamelukes, Arabs, Bedouins and Egyptians was easily defeated by a much smaller, but technologically superior French force. Thereafter the Mameluke leader, Mourad-bey, and

The Ottoman empire. *Source: Wikicommons*

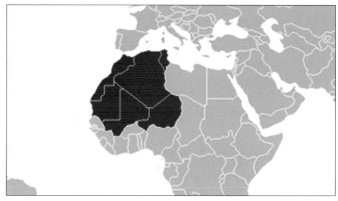

The Maghreb region: the French territories of Algeria, Morocco, Tunisia, Niger, Mali and Mauritania. *Source: Wikicommons*

his remaining army fled into the Egyptian desert pursued by advancing French troops.

All this augured well for Napoleon's oriental adventure, but abruptly the British appeared on the scene and tore down the curtain. The sole tactical weakness of the entire expedition had been the fact that British naval superiority in the Mediterranean rendered the French occupation force extremely vulnerable. The worst that could possibly happen happened between 1 and 3 August, 1798, when Admiral Horatio Nelson trapped the French fleet in Aboukir Bay, between Alexandria and the mouth of the Nile, where it was annihilated in what would come to be known as the Battle of the Nile. Napoleon suddenly found himself, along with a force of 35,000 men, trapped in Egypt.

The twenty-nine-year-old Bonaparte, with typically youthful élan, shrugged off this disaster. With little apparent regard for the consequences, he embarked on a dramatic but ill-advised conquest of Syria in an effort to destroy the Ottoman Empire and increase his domains, no doubt still clinging somewhat to the shreds of his Alexandrian dream. The French, however, confronting a combined British and Ottoman Turkish force, were stalled at Jaffa, and then stopped at Acre, before being driven back to Egypt by a combination of military defeat and bubonic plague.

Still displaying an airy refusal to acknowledge the inevitable, Napoleon wrote of the episode: "[I] am returning [to Cairo] with many prisoners and flags. I razed the ramparts of Acre. There is not a stone left standing."

A subsequent victory over a large Turkish landing force attempting to retake Egypt at Aboukir on 11 July 1799 did nothing to buoy flagging troop morale, at which point Napoleon acknowledged defeat and resolved to return to Europe. "Accustomed as I am to view the opinion of posterity as the fit reward for the pains and labours of life," he wrote, "I leave Egypt with the deepest regret. The interests of our country, her destiny, my duty, the extraordinary circumstances alone, have persuaded me to pass through enemy lines and return to Europe."

Thus Bonaparte abandoned more than 30,000 French soldiers while he and a select corps of generals slipped back across the Mediterranean to avail themselves of fresh opportunities for glory.

Although the expedition had ended in disaster, it nonetheless exerted a powerful influence on 19th-century European culture, introducing, particularly in France, a fashion for all things Egyptian. This, although further entrenching Orientalist stereotypes, nonetheless allowed Napoleon to use the academic success of the expedition to mask some of its military failures. He ordered the publication of all the recorded findings of the many scientists and scholars who had accompanied him to Egypt which were collated and combined in a huge luxury edition, published between 1809 and 1822, and circulated under the title *Description de l'Égypte*.

The *Description* was composed of some twenty volumes, containing mostly oversized engravings which were explained in accompanying textual volumes. Although a testimony to Napoleon's power and achievements, the *Description* was in fact only completed under his successor, the Bourbon, King Louis XVIII.

The next great French general to stamp his indelible mark on the African continent was, of course, Charles de Gaulle who was identified with Africa primarily through the movement of the Free French during the dark days of Vichy. The most important facet of the Free French movement was the fact that the bulk of its European manpower was drawn from France's overseas colonies, most notably Africa, and later, much of the force that it was able to wield against the retreating Italians and Germans was drawn from natives of those colonies, West Africa in particular and Senegal perhaps more than any other.

From this the seeds of an understanding were sown among the French that French liberty had survived in Africa; it was to Africa, therefore, that France owed gratitude for the retention of her national dignity and indeed her imperial authority.

It was events in Algeria, however, and the emerging nationalist activity in Morocco and Tunisia, that monopolized French attention in the immediate aftermath of the Second World War. France attempted to include North Africa in the Atlantic Alliance, arguing the importance of the Mediterranean area in the overall defence of Europe.

However, when those three principal French territories of the Maghreb—Algeria, Morocco and Tunisia—achieved independence, it was accepted that French influence in the region

The British fleet attacks the French fleet at Aboukir in the Battle of the Nile. *Source: Wikicommons*

would henceforth have to depend on carefully managed economic and diplomatic entente and not direct rule. Black Africa, on the other hand, presented a much easier model for maintaining the relevance in Africa of direct French military involvement.

Why did the French and de Gaulle in particular, place such importance on a continued military role in Africa? De Gaulle was of that rare breed of soldier-politician who was able to juxtapose military strategy against the demands of realpolitik, and also to look deep enough into the future to effectively create both.

"In five years we will have a modern, technically and scientifically advanced army, adapted to our needs and to our means," he said in 1964, at the height of France's overseas reach and at the culmination of policy that he had devised during the Second World War. "An army capable of intervening everywhere. An army that will permit us to maintain our national defence policy and a global foreign policy. An army worthy of France."[20]

Why did this mean so much? It has been argued that the national humiliation of the Vichy collaboration enlarged in the French national consciousness the need to reaffirm, for the sake of itself and its international partners, the notion of France as a great and benevolent world power. It was she, after all, alone among the great powers of Europe that had been occupied. The military dispensation in Africa that backed up this renewed imperial desire was real enough, but it was also separate somewhat from the military preoccupations of other Allied powers, and as such played a very limited global strategic role, serving only perhaps to limit the degree to which the Soviet Union was able to establish itself in West and Central Africa.

It is also true that French military power in Africa, and its application, tended on the whole to be political, underlining a sense that France was still needed on the continent as the emerging nation states of the region groped toward political maturity. It also, of course, helped to retain French trade and economic exclusivity

in a region that she still regarded as being very much within her sphere of influence. Above all, it projected the symbolic relevance of *France-Afrique* in the aftermath of the obliteration of that most important imperial residue, *Algéri française*.

On a more practical level, France was apt to argue that the strong links she maintained between the metropole and the new African states was justified, not only by the obvious political, cultural and economic interests which France maintained but because, quite simply, if France did not do it then some other power would.

The framework of French military involvement in Africa consisted of a series of military agreements entered into with the emerging nations of Francophone Africa. These were generally of two kinds: defence agreements that made available to African states the opportunity to call upon France for direct military support, and military cooperation agreements under the terms of which France undertook to provide African states with technical advisers, to absorb African students into French military schools and to transfer military material to equip and supply, usually at no cost, the *armées nationales*.

On the whole these agreements were carefully crafted to retain both French influence and her freedom of action. The French objective in this regard was to distribute military bases across the region, including Madagascar, in an interlocking security blanket that would cover the entirety of Francophone Africa. As John Chipman observed in his book, *French Power in Africa*, the French strategy sought to ensure her supply of raw materials from these countries while at the same time reserving the right to abstain from the direct involvement of French troops if she chose.[21]

Between 1960 and 1961, twelve African states signed defence agreements on various levels with France. These were: The Central African Republic, Chad, Congo, Gabon, Senegal, Madagascar, Côte d'Ivoire, Dahomey (Benin), Niger, Mauritania, Togo and Cameroon. Certain bilateral agreements were reached

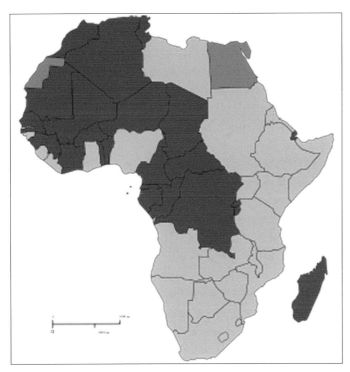

Francophone Africa.
Source: Wikicommons

French military involvement in Tunisia, January 1952.
Source: Gallo Images/Getty Images

with Mali, but it was not until 1977 that a watered-down military cooperation agreement was signed between the two countries. Upper Volta (Burkina Faso) demanded the dismantling upon independence of French bases and refused any kind of agreement, conceding only over-flight, staging and transit permissions. Only Guinea among the ex-colonial territories of the region signed no military assistance or cooperation agreements at all.

This was the exception rather than the rule, however, and in general the various military protocols reached through these agreements were welcomed, and indeed a number of African leaders sought to extend the terms to the provision of personal security in the form of presidential guards or direct technical assistance theretofore. All the countries which originally signed defence agreements, with the exception of Togo and Dahomey, in due course sought protection from France in one way or another against both external and internal threats.

These military agreements, although they played on the fears and paranoia of weak and often un-representative leaders, were in general a coup for the French in their desire to remain relevant on the continent, establishing from the onset France's right of exclusive action in Francophone Africa. This was often on her own terms, in most cases with annexure that stipulated trade and other monopolies, including, in the interests of the standardization of equipment, the requirement that signatories commit to call exclusively on France for the maintenance and renewal of matériel. These were not always strictly adhered to, but the protocol of turning to France for military assistance was established from the onset.

Thus, African soldiers were able and indeed encouraged at certain levels to serve in the French army, quite as French soldiers could serve in the armies of particular African states. This interchangeablity ensured the perpetuation of a Franco–African

solidarity that went far beyond the usual political pronouncements of shared interests and commonality characterizing the usual post-colonial north–south continuum.

Entrenched within the terms of these agreements was the strategic placement of French military bases in order to provide effective reach across the spectrum of Francophone Africa. The region was therefore divided into two strategic zones: the Indian Ocean, including Madagascar and Djibouti, and Central Africa, comprising all the ex-West and -Central African colonies.

The Central African Zone was itself divided into three *zones d'outre mer* (ZOMs) with headquarters at Dakar in Senegal, Abidjan in Côte d'Ivoire and Brazzaville in Congo. The Indian Ocean ZOM was headquartered in the Madagascan capital of Tananarive.

Five categories of facility were maintained. These were principal bases at which elements of all three branches of the armed forces were stationed, intermediate bases which the French could use to facilitate ease of movement around the continent, replacement bases which could be quickly established if a principal base was lost, security garrisons which were set up on an ad hoc basis and locations where staging rights were automatically granted. In 1960 these collectively numbered in excess of a hundred facilities scattered across the three *zones d'outre mer*, with the most important principal bases situated at Djibouti, Dakar, Diego-Suarez (Antsiranana) and Fort Lamey (N'Djamena). Other significant installations were located at Port Bouet in Côte d'Ivoire, Libreville in Gabon and of course in Bangui, the Central African Republic.

This, all in all, represented a very heavy deployment of force, a fact which was observed by many visitors to the region prior to independence, illustrated perhaps best by the observations of Geoffrey Gower, a British traveller, commenting on the French colonies of West Africa:

> Perhaps the thing which surprised me most in French West Africa was the excessive militarization of the country. In any conglomeration of any size was a barracks; and it comparatively seldom that and hour passed without hearing a military bugle. Indeed the bugle has completely ousted the tom-tom as a background to local colour.[22]

All this began to change by necessity as the process of decolonization began to take place. The reasons were partly political, obviously, but also thanks to the improvements wrought on indigenous African military formations as a consequence of French technical assistance, making it possible for African armies to carry out much of the work that had previously been undertaken by metropolitan units. Also, of course, by the latter half of the 20th century, rapid deployment by air and the establishment of support facilities on the ground in various places rendered it practical to thin out French deployments on the ground.

Technical assistance, the bureaucratic euphemism for training and equipping *armées nationales*, was undertaken by technical advisers, another euphemism, while armaments and matériel were provided by the French government. In order to facilitate this process, a Bureau d'Aide Militaire or a Mission d'Aide Militaire was established in each territory owning an agreement with the metropole. All this was coordinated at home by the French Ministry of Cooperation, formed in 1961 upon the general decolonization, much as the British Foreign and Commonwealth Office emerged in order to manage the relationship between the Crown and her ex-colonies. The defence agreements, as such, were managed directly by the Ministry of Defence.

As an indication of the level of importance attached to African cooperation, a Council of African and Malagasy Affairs was formed at more or less the same time. This consisted of the president, the prime minister, the foreign minister and the minister of cooperation. The council was short lived, eliminated by Giscard d'Estaing as an early imprint of his own foreign policy, and its functions more or less devolved to a permanent adviser at the Élysée Palace on African Affairs. This was a role that had previously been occupied during the de Gaulle period by the inimical Jacques Foccart, who was removed by Giscard in favour René Journiac, Foccart's one-time deputy, and a man more aligned to Giscard's more modern way of thinking. This naturally ensured that African policy received the maximum degree of attention and was resolved at the highest level.

In the meanwhile, troop withdrawals from Africa were balanced by the formation in 1962 of the *Force Interarmées d'Intervention*, a ground, naval and aerial intervention force created ostensibly for rapid response anywhere in the world, but poised in the south of France where prompt deployment to anywhere within the Central African Zone could easily be managed. This would naturally be a politically more viable solution than having boots on the ground in Africa, but with no real reduction in the capacity of France to act within the region.

Thus, from that period on, French military policy in Africa occupied three strata. The first were the *armées nationales* in each individual territory that had been carefully configured to be virtually interchangeable with the French army; secondly *the forces d'outre-mer,* African-based French units stationed at key points throughout Francophone Africa and which, under defence and cooperation agreements, could be used in support of local forces, and thirdly, the *Force Interarmées d'Intervention* which was able to provide rapid land, sea and air reinforcements in the event of a crisis. The operational link between the *Forces d'Outre-Mer* and the *Force Interarmées d'Intervention* was necessarily very close, bearing in mind that a rapid airborne deployment would be reliant on the forces already present on the ground securing, or being in possession of, the necessary ground facilities.

Through the mid-1960s, French forces were active in Africa in a number of instances of internal disturbance or rebellion, considered inimical to French interests and which, in political terms, led to active discussion on the impartiality of French policy making with regards to Africa. These took place at various times in Cameroon, Mauritania, Senegal, Congo, Gabon and Chad.

The most controversial of these early French interventions was that in support of dictatorial Gabonese President Gabriel Léon M'ba, by no means the most odious of his breed, but nonetheless a man wont to secure his position through the usual Machiavellian devices. When M'ba dissolved the national assembly in January 1964 to institute one-party rule, an army coup sought to oust him from power and restore parliamentary democracy. French paratroopers were on the scene within twenty-four hours with the objective of returning M'ba to power. The coup was effectively crushed and despite widespread protests and riots, the opposition was rounded up and imprisoned.

The French were subject to a certain amount of international political and press censure in the aftermath of this operation which led to an overall review of France's military policy in Africa, and an acceleration of troop withdrawals with a view to placing greater reliance on the *Force Interarmées d'Intervention*. These changes were explained to the French public largely in economic terms, but the political ramifications of French activity in the region played a clear role in the decision. French interventions in Africa to date, including the 2011 intervention to aide elected Ivorian leader Alassane Ouattara against incumbent Laurent Gbagbo in the final days of that country's effective civil war, number some twenty-five, with the most high profile being the frequent but ongoing periods of military involvement in Chad.

After 1964 French policy in Africa tended to concentrate on the principal of local technical and training assistance with a gradually diminishing level of local deployment, and of course a greater reliance on the deterrent potential of the *Force Interarmées d'Intervention*. A string of coups d'état that took place in the mid-1960s—in 1965 and 1966 alone there were coups d'état in Dahomey, the Central African Republic and Upper Volta as well as in other territories of interest to France such as Algeria, Burundi and Zaire—none of which resulted in interventions. The first major action following Gabon was the intervention in Chad in 1969, which was followed by Djibouti in 1976, Mauritania in 1977, Zaire 1977/8, Chad 1978/80 and of course Operation *Barracuda* in the Central African Republic in 1979. Others followed.

It was the arrival in power of Valéry Giscard d'Estaing in May 1974 that brought about an end to the policy of military disengagement from Africa that had been ongoing for nearly a decade. He was the first president since de Gaulle, and perhaps even more so than him, who had a personal interest in Africa. The much-publicized hunting safaris that brought Giscard so frequently to the CAR

Bureau d'Aide Militaire.
Source: Wikicommons

Laurent Gbagbo.
Source: Wikicommons

in 1978, France upstaged Belgium by deploying 600 foreign legionnaires and a hundred paratroopers directly to Kolwezi. These were followed by three more companies of troops. The French, and an additional 1,750 Belgian troops, were airlifted into the region later on aircraft borrowed from the US Military Airlift Command, using bases at Dakar and Libreville to refuel. Various other interventions in the late 1970s included the ongoing dispute over the Western Sahara which twice drew in the French. In the first instance, in December 1977, the French intervened against the Polisario Front in Mauritania to secure the release of French prisoners, followed in May 1979 by a second intervention in support of a political solution to the ongoing crisis. In June 1977 France provided logistical support to the Chadian air force in order to deal with a renewed offensive by the *Front de Libération Nationale du Tchad* (FROLINAT) in the north of that country. This was followed in April 1977 by the deployment of ground troops. And then, of course, there was Operation *Barracuda* in September 1979, consistently presented by the French as being in support of David Dacko's ouster of Bokassa, but in reality the first instance of actual regime change. This fact was met by the French press and general public with some approval—it would hardly have been appropriate to mourn the forced removal of such a prominent stain on the Franco–African landscape—but retention of troops in the country thereafter solicited much debate and no less criticism.

were also indicative of how his passion transcended politics. The effusion with which Bokassa treated the personal relationship that he enjoyed, or perhaps *thought* he enjoyed, with Giscard, was no different to the outpourings of devotion and fraternity that he had claimed with de Gaulle. Both, however, were based more on Bokassa's desire to be taken seriously than any genuine exchange of affection.

Nonetheless, the sense of an imperial French presidency stimulated by these kinds of personal links were very reminiscent of the early days of de Gaulle; it was tragic in a way that matters such as the Diamond Affair should have intruded to discredit what was in reality an important and successful foreign policy strategy.

Another such personal link that earned economic dividends for France in a questionable political environment was that between Giscard and Zairian president Mobutu Sese Seko. The two men met at the beginning of 1971 when Giscard visited Zaire, the largest French-speaking nation outside of France, in the capacity of French finance minister, initiating a personal relationship between the two that continued after Giscard's election to the presidency. Military cooperation between the two nations began in 1973, with Mobuto ordering Mirage jet fighters, Puma helicopters and other items of military hardware from France, and then in 1974 with the signing of a military assistance agreement.

Practical military assistance was, of course, not long in coming. Two military expeditions to Zaire were mounted in 1977 and 1978 in the Shaba region in support of Mobutu against the internal rebel movement, the *Front de Libération Nationale Congolaise* (FLNC). In the first instance the French stepped in when the US hesitated, attempting to smudge the clear lines of French involvement by seconding Moroccan troops in order to present the operation as an all-African affair. During the second invasion by the FLNC

This criticism was obviously based on the French decision to retain enhanced troop levels in the territory, causing many to question the true function and extent of the military intervention. French official concern was best expressed in December 1979 by veteran Gaullist politician and rival presidential candidate to Giscard, Pierre Messmer, during an animated debate in the legislative assembly.

"To be tolerable," Messener remarked, in implied sensitivity to increasing criticism of French neo-colonialism in Africa, "... any use of force in Africa must have an indispensible motive and be strictly limited in time and space, that is, brief and punctual ... the fact that their prolongation is demanded by the interested governments is an explanation that cannot satisfy us."[23]

On another occasion, perhaps liberated this time from the partisanship of the national assembly, Pierre Messmer commented more candidly, and more accurately, on the odds of David Dacko's unsupported survival in the aftermath of Barracuda: "I'm afraid he doesn't have enough character and courage." He ruefully admitted, "If the French paratroops leave tomorrow, he will probably go with them."

CHAPTER FIVE:
THE FRENCH TAKE OVER THE REPUBLIC

The French certainly did leave a strong force in Bangui to keep an eye on things in the aftermath of Operation *Barracuda*. Dacko could scarcely have survived without them; and neither could the French have allowed their intervention to be discredited by his prompt removal through a coup, or worse still, through a general election. The popular mood in the country was not positive, and neither were the memories of Dacko's earlier rule encouraging.

As the strike force of Operation *Barracuda* left the territory, French support troops settled in. The old French military bases at Bouar and Bangui were reoccupied while French 'advisers' were installed in each key ministry. Overseeing all this was the principal *barbouze*, Lieutenant-Colonel Jean-Claude Mantion, an officer of the French *Direction Générale de la Sécurité Extérieure* (DGSE).

Mantion would become an important figure during the next few years, frequently observed out and about in Bangui, officious and yet vaguely untrustworthy, most often seen wearing a pale, open-necked safari shirt with a walkie-talkie slung under his arm. He was ostensibly placed in charge of security, under which mandate he created, trained and commanded a 450-man contingent of presidential guards. These men, distinctive thanks to their red berets and with a snarling panther badge on their arms, kept watch over the Palais de la Renaissance, effectively guaranteeing, with the implied force of the French garrison behind them, the safety of the regime. Mantion, however, was ubiquitous. He swiftly acquired the nickname 'the Proconsul' thanks to the all-embracing nature of his duties. His official mandate was to protect Dacko, but in reality he controlled the administration, coordinating the technical advisers, under whom the heads of individual ministries effectively understudied, and ensured that Dacko played by the rules and respected the primacy of French interests.

In the meanwhile, political opposition to Dacko was quick to make itself felt in the form of Ange-Félix Patassé, Bokassa's first prime minister, who approached the scheduled 1981 presidential election at the head of the Movement for the Liberation of the Central African People, or MPLC, founded in January 1979. He had been energized by a groundswell of popular support based on a widespread suspicion of Dacko's return and a desire in the country for authentic change.

A presidential election, meanwhile, was scheduled for 15 March 1981. Dacko stood as the incumbent against a stable of opposition hopefuls, including Ange-Félix Patassé as arguably the most popular candidate, and Henri Maïdou and Abel Goumba as something of a supporting cast. Dacko, however, upon an extremely narrow majority, emerged victorious, and was inaugurated as president of the republic on 1 April 1981. It was widely felt, however, a position advocated strenuously by Patassé, that Dacko had been elected as a French puppet in an election engineered by the French to serve French interests. His right to

rule was skilfully challenged by Patassé, who openly intrigued against the presidency, using the powerful weapon of ethnicity in a steeply ethnocentric political environment. Patassé belonged to the largest ethnic group in the country, the Gbaya, and enjoyed residential and kinship ties with other allied groups.

There also appears to have been pressure building within the armed forces, the *Forces Armées Centrafricaines*, or FACA, which hinted at the likelihood of another military coup, pressure against which Dacko seems to have wilted. An unwilling heir to the empire, he had survived two years in office, but, in ill health, weakened by fear and paranoia, he is said to have summoned Jean-Claude Mantion and informed him that he intended to submit to a coup and voluntarily hand over power to the military, led in this instance by Chief of Staff, General André Kolingba.

Kolingba, no doubt, could hardly believe his luck, and seized upon the laurels with alacrity. History has portrayed the episode as a bloodless coup that deposed Dacko, with mention seldom made of the fact that Dacko effectively relinquished power. It has also been suggested that local security agents, possibly at Mantion's instigation, were behind the decision, an action, if this is true, that was undertaken without the direct knowledge or participation of the new socialist administration under President François Mitterrand. Mitterrand, incidentally, took power promising a complete revision of the Franco–African policy of his predecessors. A comment attributable to him:

> The historical links which unite us with Africa make of the peoples of that continent privileged partners in a cooperation which should cease to be adapted to the exigencies of local oligarchies, themselves in the services of public interests in the metropole. With the African governments, all military cooperation agreements should be renegotiated.[24]

With the parting words to Giscard that he had behaved toward Africa like a "pyromaniac fireman", Mitterrand seemed to approach the question of *Franceafrique* with an eye on the OAU, and the responsibility of Africa itself to attend to questions of African indiscipline. He appeared to have resolved to ensure that military intervention in Africa be a thing of the past.

David Dacko, in the meanwhile, temporarily left the political stage of the Central African Republic, unharmed and at liberty, which in itself lent some justification for his unusual course of action. Thereafter, General André Kolingba formed a Military Committee for National Recovery, remaining extremely close to the French, and indeed extremely close to Jean-Claude Mantion himself, which again tended to suggest that Mantion might have played a part. Indeed, Mantion transferred his loyalty from Dacko

Légionnaires of the crack 2nd REP patrolling days after the mutiny, in the rebel suburbs of Bimbo and Petovo. As tensions decrease they wear their berets; by doing so they hope to demonstrate to the population that they are not the enemy. *Source: Yves Debay*

A 20mm cannon protrudes from the door of a Puma helicopter with its gunner behind armour plating.
Source: Yves Debay

1st RPIMa. *Source: Yves Debay*

Ange-Félix Patassé.
Source: Gallo Images/Getty Images

General André Kolingba.
Source: Ministère de la Défense

Arrival of the FACA at Camp Béal.
Source: Ministère de la Défense

to Kolingba with a minimum of regret, proving his worth to the new military leader very quickly when, on 3 March 1982, he thwarted an attempted coup instigated by an aggrieved Ange-Félix Patassé, supported by two prominent FACA officers, Brigadiers François Bozizé and Alphonse Mbaïkoua.

In the aftermath of the attempt the two officers promptly fled, with Bozizé taking refuge in Chad and Mbaïkoua in his home village of Markounda, situated close to the border with Chad. Patassé, meanwhile, sought the protection of the French embassy in Bangui, which caused considerable embarrassment in Paris. His exile was negotiated by the French with an extremely surly Kolingba, and in due course Patassé found himself aboard a French military transport aircraft en route to Togo. This was not, however, to be the last that the Central African Republic would see of this energetic, ambitious and determined man.

Kolingba, meanwhile, turned out to be something of an insignificant figure, devolving much of the power of state to the chief *barbouze*, Jean-Claude Mantion, or 'Lucky Luke' as he was known in certain quarters, in whom he had invested a great deal of trust and confidence. Through Mantion, however, the French continued to steer the ship of state in their own direction, keeping a steady hand on the wheel, and allowing Kolingba the latitude only to attend to what was important to him. This, of course, was to ethnically align his government and the local security services, in particular the FACA, with members of his own Yakoma group. The Yakoma are a minority constituent of the CAR demographic, centred on the north bank of the Ubangi, and making up only four per cent of the general population.

And in an action that would have ramification deep into the future, Kolingba also embarked on a program of ethnic cleansing, using loyal Yakoma elements in the military to mount punitive raids in the north of the country during which the usual toll of rape, pillage and murder was exacted. Many analysts point to this as the moment that an effective north/south divide was wrought that defined the nation as either people of the river or people of the savannah. In future almost every domestic disturbance, be it political or social, would have about it an ethnic tone. This, in of itself, was sufficient catalyst to ensure ongoing insecurity,

notwithstanding the enormous economic and social pressures being brought to bear by the mismanagement attributable to Bokassa and added to by each successive political generation.

In the meanwhile, the 1980s drew to a close, and the Eastern Bloc collapsed. Old Cold War certainties that had allowed patently corrupt leaders across the region to survive through superpower

François Bozizé.
Source: Wikicommons

patronage evaporated, ushering in an era of aid and foreign support conditional on democratic reforms. This sounded the death knell for many regimes across Africa and although Kolingba was hardly one of the heavy hitters in this league, as Bokassa had been, he recognized the practical ramifications of his position, and ceded with a minimum of resistance to what the French press dubbed 'Paristroika'.

In April 1991 Kolingba conceded to multiparty elections that he stood no chance of winning. With a degree of candour unusual in politics, he remarked during an interview on national radio: "I did it because those who pay us asked me to."[25]

And so it was. Needless to say the journey toward democracy in the CAR followed a course prescribed by Paris. Elections were organized and closely monitored and were as a consequence judged to be indisputably fair. And who should emerge as victor but Ange-Félix Patassé, returning from exile to seize the laurels; this man who had occupied varied and often contradictory roles. How would this play out for Paris in a new age of political transparency?

Patassé had at times been virulently anti-French, he had been a coup master, had arranged the coronation of a faux emperor and had lately been touring the villages promising each one a machine that manufactured banknotes should he win.[26] It was certainly with great misgivings that Paris watched the process unfold and inevitably, compelled by the pressures of their own foreign policy, the French were forced to accept and live with the result.

Comité Français de la Libération Nationale. Source: Wikicommons

President Léopold Senghor of Senegal and members of his party are welcomed upon their arrival in the United States for a visit.
Source: Wikicommons

The Battle of the Nile. *Source: Wikicommons*

President Félix Houphouët-Boigny and his wife, Marie-Thérèse, 22 May 1962.
Source: Wikicommons

Napoleon Bonaparte in Egypt.
Source: Wikicommons

Portrait of Louis XVIII in coronation robes (he was never crowned). *Source: Wikicommons*

President Ahmed Sékou Touré of Guinea arrives for a visit to Washington D.C.
Source: Wikicommons

Jean-Bédel Bokassa.
Source: Wikicommons

Right: 2nd RPIMa in Bangui.
Photo: Yves Debay

Below: Marines of 3rd RPIMa
patroling the deserted centre of
Bangui. *Photo: Yves Debay*

3rd RPIMa on patrol in Bangui
Photo: Yves Debay

A ferry on a tributary of the Oubangui river under the watchful eye of 1st RPIMa. *Photo: Yves Debay*

2nd REP checkpoint. *Photo: Yves Debay*

French marines of the 1st RPIMa patroling with a Peugeot P-4 and an AML-90 in the centre of Bangui. *Photo: Yves Debay*

Presidential Guard. *Photo: Yves Debay*

An RCA Presidential Guardsman with an RPG-7. *Photo: Yves Debay*

A Mirage F1 CR during *Almandin*. *Photo: Yves Debay*

Left and right: EUFOR peacekeeping force in Chad. *Source: Ministerstwo Obrony Narodowej*

The town of Birao in northern CAR was largely razed during fighting in 2007. *Source: Wikicommons*

Cameroonian Navy sailors board the French surveillance frigate, FS *Germinal* F735, to practise a RECAMP search-and-seizure drill, Douala, Cameroon. *Source: Wikicommons*

Military exercises in the area of *Camp Aeromobile* Am Nabak, where Polish soldiers are stationed in Chad. These operations are to enhance security in the Sudanese refugee camps.
Source: Ministerstwo Obrony Narodowej

CHAPTER SIX:
DEMOCRACY AND MUTINY

The optimism that greeted this new era of transparency would prove very quickly to be misplaced. The legacy of thirty years of maladministration could hardly be swept away by the occasion of a free and fair ballot. The seeds of chaos had been deeply planted and were tribal in character, producing a tree of a type that inevitably grows strong and resilient in Africa.

Prior to this, three indigenous leaders had stood astride the republic. All three had been ethnically aligned to the south. Ange-Félix Patassé was the first to originate from the north. This of itself had little bearing but upon the perception that the traditionally marginalized northerners, the people of the savannah, would now be promoted above the southerners, the people of the river, which, of course, presented the potential for deep polarization, a potential that Patassé did nothing to diminish. In fact, whether by accident or design, Patassé did more than any other to aggravate it.

Patassé inherited a military and security apparatus that had been transformed by Kolignba into an effective tribal militia. The predominance of Yakoma in the armed forces, and most importantly in the Presidential Guard—that thin line of security that all unstable leaders maintain between themselves and their population—was a source of deep disquiet to the new president.

At first Patassé attempted to neutralise this concentration by transferring Yakoma from the Presidential Guard, the *Unité de Sécurité Présidentielle*, to the ranks of the FACA, which, bearing in mind an abrupt reduction in terms of service, became an immediate source of anger and discontent. This was further inflamed by subsequent moves to do precisely as his predecessor had done and pack the presidential security force with members of his own ethnic group, the Sara-Kaba, concentrated primarily in the north.

The rivalry that immediately took root between the elite and somewhat pampered Presidential Guard and the ramshackle units of the FACA would prove to be the catalyst for a series of violent mutinies that would prove the depressing continuum of unreliable government and draw the French once more into the vortex of instability in the Central African Republic.

The first mutiny took place on 18 April 1996, and came on the back of ongoing civil servant and teachers strikes. This involved between 200 and 300 soldiers of the Operational Defence of the Territory Regiment, the *Régiment de Défense Opérationnelle du Territoire*, demonstrating in support of demands for the payment of three months of unpaid wages. Armed mutineers entered the city in vehicles, seizing additional weapons and vehicles from a police station. Soldiers then occupied the main fuel depot, the radio station, taking a number of prominent officials hostage and forcing their way past guards at the main prison where cells were ordered opened, sending convicts streaming into the city. Witnesses said mutineers also entered the homes of business executives, demanding money and vehicles and beating those who refused. Rebels then attempted to attack the presidential palace while Patassé himself took temporary refuge in the nearby French army base. The attackers were immediately confronted by the Presidential Guard in a clash which left nine men dead, including four members of the Presidential Guard, and an estimated forty wounded. Five civilians were killed. Defence Minister Jean Mette-Yapende went on state radio to promise that troops would be paid immediately, urging the mutineers to return to their barracks.

In what was termed Operation *Almandin I*, French soldiers based at the nearby Béal military base occupied key installations in the city and, ostensibly alongside loyal elements, patrolled Bangui to protect foreign nationals. French mediators, meanwhile, helped negotiate an end to the mutiny. The French agreed to pay the wage arrears while Patassé agreed to a general amnesty. All told the mutiny lasted for three days.

A month later a second mutiny erupted, this time over an attempt by Patassé to place the main armoury under the control of the Presidential Guard. On Saturday, 18 May 1996, some 500 soldiers, led on this occasion by non-commissioned officers of the FACA, flooded out onto the streets of Bangui demanding the payment of back wages and control of the national armoury. A feature of this episode that differed from the previous was the extent and severity of the violence, but also the fact that alongside the usual demands for payments were other, more political stipulations that included the resignation of Patassé himself and an end to the almost absolute domination of the local political establishment by the French. Indeed, the deployment of the 1,300 or so French troops stationed in the country was immediate, with additional forces being flown in from Gabon and Chad.

It was also not too long before the political demands of the mutiny prompted a more general series of strikes, which in turn precipitated further looting and general lawlessness. Within a very short time the capital began to resemble a war zone. The French immediately opened negotiations with the mutineers, bypassing the government which, although it came as something of a relief to Patassé, also tended to add grist to the mill of anti-French feeling in the capital.

By 20 March French troops were a highly visible presence on the streets, supported by tanks and armoured cars. Efforts by the mutineers, by then numbering some 500, to take the radio station were thwarted by a French helicopter gunship that attacked and killed nine government troops in a vehicle. Two days later US Marines, fresh from a similar operation in Liberia, appeared in support of French efforts to centralize and evacuate foreign nationals. In the case of the US nationals, these were primarily Peace Corps workers located in and around the capital. France was thanked by the United States for rescuing a small group of Peace

Arrival of the rebels at the National Assembly.
Source: Ministère de la Défense

Evacuation of French nationals from Bangui.
Source: Ministère de la Défense

Corps volunteers caught in the crossfire in downtown Bangui. Those expatriates serving in the outlying areas tended to be aloof from the focus of violence and were not deemed to be in any particular danger.

By 26 May, almost a week after the start of the mutiny, the systematic looting of the city, by then almost completely destroyed, moved toward the more affluent suburbs on the north bank of the Ubangi river, where most senior diplomatic residences were located. Across the wide expanse of the river, small craft could be seen moving backward and forward ferrying large amounts of looted property across the river into Zaire. American official residences were comprehensively ransacked, as were the residences of the local World Bank representatives, before looters were chased off by patrolling French troops. The French cultural centre, the most visible sign of the French presence in downtown *Bangui*, was destroyed by fire after French troops, along with loyal elements of the FACA, had fired warning shots at demonstrators. A senior western diplomat was heard to observe: "What we are seeing, unfortunately, is just a total breakdown of law and order."[27]

In the devastated city centre French troops, by then numbering some 3,000, sheltered in defensive positions behind the bullet-ridden walls of homes and businesses destroyed in the looting, while hundreds of anti-government and anti-French protesters marched for a third consecutive day, defying a ban on public gatherings, and angrily denouncing the French presence in the country. Visible from French positions, meanwhile, FACA mutineers also clung to their static fortifications, wary, heavily armed and on the defensive. A reported twelve FACA soldiers had been killed thus far, although this was probably a conservative estimate, and an indeterminate number of civilians, all against a confirmed two French soldiers injured.

Close to Bangui international airport, adjacent to France's main local air base, a second march was organized, this time in favour of the government, but comprising a conspicuously smaller crowd and lacking much of the passion of the anti-government demonstration.

For the French, the mutiny presented a very delicate military and political conundrum. A statement issued from Paris by

Cooperation Minister Jacques Godfrain admitted that what had initially been planned as a military intervention to protect and evacuate French civilians had devolved into an intervention to prop up the government of Ange-Félix Patassé. "The mission is to maintain the democratic state," he said, "... that means freedom of movement and freedom of expression."

It had been the self-same Godfrain, before fielding passionate appeals from Patassé for an intervention, who had earlier stated that France would not intervene in the CAR except in an instance of external aggression. "We are not the gendarmes of Africa," M. Godfrain stated.

Such was the view from the Élysée Palace. Locally, however, the situation was fraught with difficulty. French involvement in the crisis was seen in many quarters, and not least on the streets of France, as symptomatic of persistent efforts by France to retain almost complete control of affairs of state in the Central African Republic and indeed in many other parts of Africa. In an interview conducted by a local reporter braving the streets, an anti-French demonstrator was quoted as saying: "What we were living was a disguised colonialism ... in every office where anything is decided here, you find a Frenchman. But these events represent an end of that era."

The end it may have been, but events as they continued to unfold in Liberia spoke of even more ghastly possibilities. France had never before encountered such a dramatic display of hostility to its role in Central Africa, prompting many to ponder whether this was in fact simply a continuation of the popular struggle for independence that had begun three decades earlier. France had never, it seemed, really granted sovereignty to the nation and many of the deeper scars—Bokassa, Dacko, Kolingba and now Patassé—had been caused by French interference and refusal to permit any kind of self-determination that might interfere with French interests.

This may have been so, but such headlines as "African quicksand" that screamed off the pages of French newspapers revealed the depth of the conundrum. To remain engaged in the internal affairs of the CAR, in particular militarily, lent fuel to arguments that the French were engaged in a neo-imperialist agenda. Evacuating

Anti-French grafitti in Bangui.
Source: Ministère de la Défense

French troops, however, to appease a growing wave of anti-French feeling in the republic, would simply have opened the way for a descent into the kind of chaos as had so recently been witnessed in Liberia, Rwanda and Burundi. "In more than three decades of independence, the Central African Republic has only known a few brief, bright moments of democracy and stability," commented an editorial in *Libération*, "and France, deeply associated with this history, has scarcely harvested any glory."

In the meanwhile, and once again, negotiations were taken up by the French independently of the government; in this instance between FACA rebel leader, Sergeant Cyriac Souké, and a high-ranking French general, Bernard Thorette. Thorette had been flown into the country from Paris, along with his staff, a hundred special forces commandos and twenty-four armoured personnel carriers, arriving early on Thursday, 23 May 1996. Wednesday had also seen the bulk of French reinforcements arriving in the capital.

Prior to the arrival of General Thorette, the political demands being made had been broadly confined to the resignation of key defence aides to Ange-Félix Patassé, but as the rebellion degenerated into civil unrest, which itself overspilled the boundaries of Bangui and began to be felt in the countryside, demands began to be heard for the removal of Patassé himself and the resignation of his entire government.

Clearly, as far as the French were concerned, this was not on the table. The French had overseen, and indeed guaranteed, free and fair elections, and Ange-Félix Patassé, for better or worse, had been the result. However, a vociferous but loosely focused opposition, with a number of important names jostling for prominence, was increasingly making itself heard. The most strident voice was that of Abel Goumba. Unusually within the club of African politicians, Goumba enjoyed a reputation for honesty and an apparent commitment to democracy. He had suffered defeat at the polls by both Dacko and Patassé, and perhaps within this context recognized an opportunity for himself. He was, however, virulently anti-French, which, under the circumstances, was perhaps ill advised.

Patassé, meanwhile, responding to the inevitable, announced during a televised broadcast on Friday 24 May that he would form a new government that would include members of the opposition. This, he hoped, would blunt the more general opposition. He also suggested a repeat of the earlier amnesty. By then, however, Bangui was in ruins. The French had concentrated and surrounded the remaining mutineers in Camp Kassai, their main barracks outside Bangui, and the capital was under a dusk-to-dawn curfew enforced by the French. A conservative estimate put the dead at that point at forty-three, with some 300 reported wounded. Hospitals, however, had been inundated, suggesting a far greater death toll; indeed the capital remained strewn with uncollected dead.

By the end of the weekend the situation had stabilized somewhat which gave Patassé a little room to manoeuvre, but only a little. Matters still resided between the French and the mutineers and on Sunday, 26 May a peace agreement was signed that resulted in the formation of a government of national unity, headed by intellectual writer and politician Jean-Paul Ngoupandé, appointed prime minister by Patassé on 6 June.

This government survived for eight months, during which Jean-Paul Ngoupandé was mandated with the almost impossible task of organizing a national conference on military reform in preparation for an overhaul of the FACA, and to get all the political parties, some thirty in all, to agree to a minimum common program.

Patassé, however, with his own agenda, sought now to marginalize the army, by then a force both hostile to himself and increasingly a danger to the republic. Reacting to this and the usual grievances of pay and conditions, a third mutiny erupted on 15 November 1996, which naturally derailed any effect that the unity government might have had. This time unrest was more widespread and less easy to contain. Moreover, it took place against the wider spectre of conflict beginning to occur between the southern Yakoma represented by the Yakoma-dominated armed forces, and Patassé's own Baya group from the north, supported by civilian militias aided by Patassé and Chadian mercenaries. Killings and abduction were increasingly reported on both sides.

Ethnic overtones to the mutiny were enlarged in the capital when, on 5 December 1996, gunmen loyal to Patassé, possibly the Presidential Guard, abducted Yakoma interior minister Christophe Grelombe and his son, both of whom were tortured before being decapitated and their bodies left in the grounds of the presidential palace.

Two days later the tempo of the mutiny was altered decisively by the killing of two French soldiers escorting regional negotiators, this time from Gabon, Mali, Chad and Burkina Faso, and termed 'mediators', to a meeting with rebels. The French response was immediate, violent and angry. Retaliations were ordered; the French struck rebel headquarters the following night, 8 December, killing ten and turning over thirty more to the authorities to meet a grim but certain fate.

In France the outcry was immediate. Many newspapers pointed out that French troops were fighting against the wrong side, bearing in mind that the mutiny was against a feeble and impoverished regime incapable of any kind of self-sustaining action, and only in existence thanks to ongoing French military

Fron left: Sergeant Souké, the Bishop of Bangui and General Thorette.
Source: Ministère de la Défense

Insurgents regroup at Camp Kassai.
Source: Ministère de la Défense

support. Concern was also expressed that by this action France had effectively taken sides in the conflict.

French president Jacques Chirac defended the decision to order retaliatory action, pointing out that passivity would simply have left the impression that French soldiers were fair game for anyone. And besides this, the French had taken sides before and had been so deeply involved in the affairs of the republic that fraternity in one direction or another was inevitable.

'The aim of this French operation was solely an act of self-defence against two particularly cowardly murders," a French foreign ministry spokesman said in Paris. "Our aim is not to put down the mutineers; our aim is to ensure that the Central African Republic can continue its democratic process."

"This is not a country, it is a dependency,' commented *le Figaro* from Bangui. "Here France is everything. Officially no one will admit it, but some fictions are deliberately preserved and Central Africa is one of them."

A French military spokesman in Bangui told reporters that French troops had taken control of the city's port facilities, fuel supplies and a short-wave radio transmitter. However, the mutineers still controlled the south of the city, the main fuel depot and the Kassai barracks.

Although hardly as overtly, France continued to maintain what many would have considered an unhealthy interest in Africa in general. Indeed, during the 1990s the French were more active on the continent than any other ex-colonial power; they continued to hold and act upon muscular defence agreements that provided France with military bases in seven other Francophone republics: Gabon, Senegal, Côte d'Ivoire, Togo, Comoros, Cameroon and Djibouti. In 1992 some 1,000 French troops had once again come to the aid of an ailing and discredited Mobuto Sese Seko as ongoing riots by unpaid soldiers threatened this regime.

Such accusations, however, were blunted in the matter of the CAR mutinies by a regional arbitration that for once did not directly involve the French. Mediators, including presidents and high-ranking officials from Mali, Gabon, Chad and Burkina Faso, remained locked in negotiations with rebel and opposition leaders after a ceasefire and truce was declared in early December.

Mediators pressed for a plan embracing amnesties, restoration of constitutional legality and an African peacekeeping force of 500 soldiers from Burkina Faso, Chad, Gabon, Mali, Senegal and Togo. All this came against a background of a Francophone summit that was held in Ouagadougou, Burkina Faso, between 4 and 6 December. Featured on the agenda were threats to the territorial integrity of Zaire, political instability in the Central African Republic and the imposition of quasi-military rule in Niger, all of which further called into question France's role in Africa. Moreover Patassé, through his minister of foreign affairs, submitted a formal request for assistance from those present in negotiating a peace accord.

In the meanwhile, French reprisals on the streets of Bangui continued, claiming an indeterminate number of lives, exacerbating local disquiet and speeding the eventual denouement that was inevitable over the matter of the French troop deployments in the CAR. The domestic mood was picked up by the then first secretary of the French Socialist party, Lionel Jospin, who delivered a speech on the matter that is widely regarded as defining the point of rupture. Jospin condemned the intervention as belonging to some past era, underlining a general feeling within France that the republic's foreign policy in regard to Africa urgently required review.

> The problem is knowing what missions our government is entrusting to our soldiers. The defence agreement with the Central African Republic, which is invoked here, is not a policing arrangement. The French army cannot be transformed either into an internal security force or a presidential guard for President Patassé.

That Patassé had won a popular vote was not in doubt, but neither was the fact that his subsequent behaviour had been less than democratic. Alongside the regional mediators grappling to find a solution, Jospin suggested an election to decide the matter. The French, in the meanwhile, faced a Cornelian choice: should it retreat from any involvement and stand to be criticized for abandoning a democratically elected president long known to

Checkpoint: 8th RPIMa and an RCA loyalist, armed with an MAS-49 rifle *Source: Yves Debay*

CRAP 2nd REP, or Pathfinder group of the elite French airborne unit. It is now called the GCP, for obvious reasons. *Source: Yves Debay*

Jacques Chirac.
Source: Ministère de la Défense

be fundamentally anti-French, or should it assume the role of the policeman of Africa and run to the assistance of Patassé, despite his abysmal record of human rights abuses, corruption and political assassination.

On 25 January 1997, the Bangui Peace Accord was signed after extensive mediation provided by a number of regional heads of state. The agreement provided for the deployment of an inter-African military mission to act as a buffer between mutineers and loyalists. The force was to be called the *Mission Interafricaine de Surveillance des Accords de Bangui*, or MISAB. Financial and logistical support would be provided by France, but command of the operation would be African.

Thus France was able to put some distance between herself and the military frontline, although she was hardly out of the picture.

CHAPTER SEVEN:
INTERNATIONAL INTERVENTION

The Bangui Peace Accord of 25 January 1997 provided for the deployment of an inter-African military mission as a buffer between mutineers and loyalists. This was the *Mission Interafricaine de Surveillance des Accords de Bangui*, or MISAB, the first authentic effort at replacing the French *Elements Français d'Assistance Operationelle*, or EFAO, with a multinational, African and most importantly an ostensibly bipartisan military presence in the Central African Republic.

The MISAB mandate, signed in Bangui on 27 January 1997, by President Bongo of Gabon, defined the objective of operation as to help restore peace and security by monitoring the implementation of the agreements signed in Bangui on 25 January. The rules of engagement were vague, but allowed MISAB to conduct what were termed lawful operations to disarm ex-rebels, the militia and other unlawfully armed individuals.[28]

Troop contributions to the force were drawn from the four African countries represented on the International Monitoring Committee that had overseen negotiations and would continue to oversee the implementation. Additional troops were provided by Senegal and Togo. Each territory provided an infantry company of roughly equal number. This strength remained more or less constant throughout the mission, numbering between 700 and 800 troops. Political authority over the mission was held by the chair of the International Monitoring Committee, Malian ex-president Amadou Toumani Touré.

All six troop-contributing countries were represented at the senior staff level. The first force commander of MISAB was Brigadier-General Dejo Edourd Nkili of Gabon, replaced in August 1997 by General Augustin Mombo Moukangi, also from Gabon. Needless to say, the entire operation was dependent on France for finance, logistics and tactical support. Although each of the contributing nations provided its troops with their regular pay, and supplied them with weapons, France met the cost of food and

daily subsistence. The French also provided all tactical and support vehicles, fuel and maintenance, rents for administrative offices and all related equipment. It was estimated by the International Monitoring Committee that the cost to France of sustaining the operation amounted to some US$600,000 per month.

In addition to this, the French provided from among the 1,300 troops permanently stationed in the CAR a logistical support command of eighty-eight personnel and a thirty-nine-man liaison and assistance detachment.

In the official declarations that accompanied the mission it was widely regarded as being a success. It did succeed in curtailing the mutiny, although in truth by then the affair was dying a natural death. Some 96 per cent of known illegal heavy armament was recovered and some 60 per cent of light weapons.

The only violent incident of any consequence to take place occurred between May and June 1997, with the death of a Senegalese soldier killed in a confrontation with mutineers. Brutal retaliations took place with, it is reported, the assistance of the French in their support capacity.[29] The character of this reaction was rather indiscriminate, with the bombing of several neighbourhoods of Bangui with artillery and mortars and a number of random, extra-judicial killings that all told exacted the highest cost in human lives since the beginning of the crisis. Red Cross estimates suggested a death toll of 500 and the dislocation of between 60,000 and 70,000 people. Human rights abuses were, of course, widely reported. The MISAB high command attempted to distance itself from the more overt atrocities committed, suggesting rather hopefully that rebels and civilians had committed crimes while wearing MISAB uniforms.

During the course of the MISAB operation, changes had taken place in France in respect of the defence accord that had for so long permitted the permanent deployment of troops in the territory. Interest in the continued support for the government of

Ange-Félix Patassé was waning. The internal security situation had grown even more complex, with Patassé naturally bypassing any involvement with FACA, and instead creating semi-official militias tasked with both the business of containing increasing ethnic insecurity in the north of the country and attending to his personal security. These took on an overt ethnic identity, augmented by mercenaries from Chad, recruited with the help of French Captain Paul Barril, the former number two of the Élysée anti-terrorist unit and a man with an extensive reputation.

In the meanwhile, when French president Jacques Chirac succeeded François Mitterrand in 1995, a debate surrounding the future of the French armed forces in a post-Cold War world began. This would see radical structural reforms, ultimately leading to the suspension of conscription, the professionalization of the armed forces in a more compact form and the reorganization of the reserve and active forces. American defence analyst and Mitterrand biographer, Ronald Tiersky, put it succinctly in his article 'French Military Reform and Restructuring': "No longer will typical operations consist of a few hundred soldiers jerry-dispatched to former French Africa to put down a coup or replace a failing president."

This was indeed to be the case, and on the back of military reforms, the decision was made to close down the two principal French military bases in Bouar and Bangui and withdraw French units deployed in the country. Bearing this news was French Minister of Defence Alain Richard who travelled to Bangui to personally inform President Ange-Félix Patassé. The impact of the withdrawal, it was hoped, would be ameliorated by the retention of some seventy military advisers to continue the work of training the FACA, but it is unlikely that Patassé was persuaded toward any other interpretation than the fact that he was being abandoned.

No mention was being made of any similar withdrawals from Chad, where the French intervention against Libya, codenamed Opération *Épervier*, or *Sparrowhawk*, had been ongoing since 1978. Patassé mulled over the implications of this withdrawal, alternately threatening the French with expulsion and appealing to the United States to fill the vacuum. In the end, however, he did nothing to interfere with or aid the withdrawal, accepting the 200 or so French troops at M'poko base outside Bangui who would remain in the country in support of MISAB and to await the deployment of a full United Nations peacekeeping force to replace it.

MISAB was succeeded in April 1998 by a UN mission, *Mission des Nations Unies en RCA*, or MINURCA. The deployment comprised some 1,350 troops and military support personnel and twenty-four civilian police, supported by international and local civilian staff. There was also a provision for 114 international civilian staff, 111 local staff and thirteen United Nations volunteers. The force was commanded by Major-General Barthélémy Ratanga (Gabon) overseeing troop contributions from Benin, Burkina Faso, Cameroon, Canada, Chad, Côte d'Ivoire, Egypt, France, Gabon, Mali, Portugal, Senegal, Togo and Tunisia.

Formal declaration by heads of state concerning the end of the mutiny. *Source: Ministère de la Défense*

The mandate of this force, as stated by the Security Council, was, inter alia, to assist in maintaining and enhancing security and stability, including freedom of movement in Bangui and the immediate vicinity of the city.[30] It was also directed to assist national security forces in maintaining order and in protecting key installations in the capital, also to "supervise . . . the final disposition of all weapons retrieved in the course of the disarmament exercise".[31]

Unmentioned in the UN resolution mandating the force was the fact that the disarmament in question had already been carried out by French troops in an earlier unilateral operation. Had that not been the case, the United States would almost certainly have refrained from taking part in MINURCA, bearing in mind the bitter controversy that had accompanied its disarmament in Somalia.

At this point, meanwhile, the 200 French soldiers remaining in Bangui swapped their berets for the blue UN helmet, causing some caustic comment within the country that the French had become "Barracudas in disguise". The situation in the capital nonetheless stabilized sufficiently for the French to now disengage completely, and on 28 February 1999 the last French soldier was airlifted out of the CAR capital.

The deployment of MINURCA was on the whole uneventful. Under its supervision a legislative elective was held in November/December 1998, which was won by the opposition, prompting President Ange-Félix Patassé to simply bypass the legislature and rule by decree. Additional short-term and medium-term United Nations staff and observers were deployed during these elections and again during the September 1999 presidential elections, which were, incidentally, won by Patassé. It is also noteworthy that ex-military leader André Kolingba lost only narrowly.

The question marks that inevitably hung over these elections were brushed aside with the usual airy tunnel-vision of the United Nations. An official communiqué remarked thus:

> MINURCA contributed significantly to restoring a climate of stability and security as well as dialogue among political actors. This progress encouraged efforts, with

Capt Paul Barril.
Source: The Biggerpicture/ Reuters

Malian president, Amadou Toumani Touré.
Source: Wikicommons

Troops in their firing positions at observation post 'Lilias' in Kalait during Operation *Épervier*.
Source: Ministère de la Défense

support of Bretton Woods institutions, to re-launch the economy and also enabled legislative elections to take place in a peaceful manner in November/December 1998. MINURCA also played a supportive role in the staging of the presidential elections of September 1999, which were won by the incumbent President Patassé.[32]

The outcome of the September presidential elections were considered sufficiently acceptable to allow for the early termination of MINURCA which took place on 1 April 2000, leaving in its place the UN peace-building office in the Central African Republic (BONUCA) with some seventy civilians and no military backup. This operation was linked to the UN department of political affairs and was primarily intended, among other things, to engage in police training and human rights seminars.

Crisis, however, remained close to the surface. Many of the basic social conditions that had precipitated the crisis of the last few years remained unresolved. The government was destitute and, once again, the payment of civil service wages were some thirty months in arrears. Opposition parties supported a strike by civil servants that endured for almost five months. By the end of 2000 renewed calls for the resignation of Patassé were being heard "in the greater interests of the nation".

That a man such as Ange-Félix Patassé should harbour any sentimentality toward the well-being of his nation was as absurd as expecting his resignation on purely moral grounds. Inevitably the situation manifested itself in opportunism and violence, and on the evening of 27/28 May a spirited attack was launched against the residence of President Patassé by a heavily armed commando that was narrowly repulsed after an intense firefight. Thereafter clashes continued throughout the city, in the midst of which frustrated presidential candidate André Kolingba announced on national radio that it had been he who had launched the coup attempt.

Much curious speculation surrounded this very public admission of responsibility for a failed coup. Local analysts suggested that Kolingba was "beleaguered" and had been "pushed to the front" by younger officers, such as General Ngjengbot, Colonel Gamba, his own son Lieutenant-Colonel Guy-Serge Kolingba and a certain Major Saulet. Whether this was the case or not, Kolingba and a number of his close associates, about twenty officers in all, were condemned to death in absentia in an August 2002 tribunal, held some time after Kolingba had entered exile in Uganda.

On the streets of Bangui, in the meanwhile, the reaction to the verdict was immediate. Government supporters were unleashed in an orgy of ethnic violence. Gangs of armed youth patrolled the streets, flushing out anyone suspected of Yakoma ethnicity or opposition sympathies. At least 300 people were reported killed in the disturbances and some 50,000 residents of the capital forced to flee. Ange-Félix Patassé narrowly survived the episode, and in fact thereafter owed his presidency to the ubiquitous Colonel Gaddafi who sent a hundred Libyan soldiers to Bangui to shore him up. In addition some 300 combatants of the *Mouvement pour la Libération du Congo* (MLC), a rebel group in neighbouring DRC, crossed the Ubangi river and made themselves available. Despite this, Patassé was quite understandably riven with paranoia, suspecting plots everywhere and enemies all around him, including, and most particularly, among the opposition. In the meanwhile, the Conglolese MLC rebels joined in the general mayhem of looting and murder, quite as the seeds of a new rebellion were planted by the hand of sacked army chief of staff François Bozizé ...

A Transall C-160.
Source: Wikicommons

A blurred image of an SPLA child soldier.
Source: Wikicommons

Puma helicopter of the 5the RHC (*Regiment d' Hélicoptères de Combat*). *Source: Yves Debay*

CHAPTER EIGHT:
THE BOZIZÉ COUP

The turn of the 21st century seemed to offer little hope for Africa. It was then that the bleak term 'Afro-pessimism' was coined by an aid-fatigued international community. In March 1999 eight foreign tourists were hacked to death by unidentified armed men in the Bwindi National Park in Uganda. A tidal wave of HIV infections seemed likely to wipe out an entire generation in southern and central Africa. In February 2000 tropical cyclone *Eline* struck the coast of Mozambique, dragging in its wake unprecedented destruction.

During the South African rescue the iconic incident of a stricken villager, Carolina Mabuiango, giving birth in a tree surrounded by mile upon mile of crocodile-infested floodwater, enthralled television viewers worldwide.

Robert Mugabe launched the land grabs that would see Zimbabwe plummet to the lower register of African failed states, quickly followed by Zimbabwe's involvements in an implosion of staggeringly violent ethnic conflict in the eastern DRC that at one time or another sucked in all the major regional players. At the same time the horror-filled tableau of child soldiers engaged in an orgy of drugs, violence and bloodshed was painted for a weary world in Liberia. Warlord politics gripped the region, toppling neighbouring Sierra Leone into perhaps one of the most awful bouts of fratricidal bloodletting recorded in any African country thus far.

Against this melancholy backdrop events in the Central African Republic seemed relatively subdued. However, the repeating pattern of rebellion and counter-rebellion, with all its associated symptoms of violence, arbitrary bloodshed and human dislocation, had very much taken root. In the aftermath of the failed coup of May 2001, President Ange-Félix Patassé succumbed to a debilitating paranoia, sensing betrayal everywhere, and finding a fresh plot around every corner.

In this regard he was ill informed only on the specifics. The steady alienation of those not ethnically aligned to him served to ensure that he did indeed have enemies everywhere, and among his friends there were few with any policy objectives more noble than rapid personal enrichment while the going was good. The absence of any meaningful French deployment in the country, meanwhile, and the unlikelihood of any further intervention, left the field open to all comers.

It was inevitable under these circumstances that Patassé would begin to make erratic and ill informed decisions. One of these was the dismissal and arrest of his minister of defence, Jean-Jacques Démafouth, a man who at one time had been very much a partner in crime and arguably one of few authentic loyalists within an extremely unreliable cabinet. Démafouth, along with many others, was detained and charged with complicity in the failed coup of March 2001. He was tried along with some 680 other defendants similarly charged, out of which only forty-nine walked free, one being him.

A corollary effect of Démafouth's detention and trial was deep disquiet felt within the ranks of the traditionally restive FACA. Although he was by no means aloof from the evils of government at that time and no less corrupt and dishonest than any other, Démafouth had been successful in restructuring the FACA to diffuse somewhat the see-saw of ethic predominance that had tended to make it so unstable. As part of this programme he had reduced the presidential security force from 1,200 to 800 men and the FACA itself by a quarter, down to about 3,000 soldiers, before then attempting to address the delicate question of ethnicity within the force. In May 2001 the percentage of soldiers from the river—essentially, the Yakoma—had been reduced to no more than 40 per cent, compared to the 70 per cent that had been the case at the end of the Kolingba regime. He had also succeeded in paying wages and had even attempted to address arrears which had softened the attitude of the army toward the government significantly.

These reforms, difficult and very skilfully wrought, had paid significant dividends when it counted. In the aftermath of the failed coup attempt the FACA had remained loyal to Patassé, and indeed had been largely responsible for his survival.

Patassé, however, was beyond any rational evaluation of the facts by then. He suspected that Démafouth was either complicit in the original coup attempt or had been instrumental in the planning of a coup within the coup. In this he was probably wrong but he could well have been right. No clear evidence existed but there was also no reason to suppose that a man at the head of the defence ministry would not be tempted to use the facilities at his disposal to effect a personal bid for power.

During his trial the French press printed a flippant and somewhat Machiavellian quote attributed to Démafouth which, of course, he fervently disowned, but which was suggestive of some sort of ambition: "I could shoot Patassé," he is reported to have said. "I have access to his bedroom. What would France offer me?"

At that time France had absolutely nothing to offer and consequently an unfortunate Démafouth took his place in the dark belly of Ngaragba prison among the ghosts of so many others and from which he could count himself very fortunate for later emerging alive.

By the time he did, however, and by the time of his acquittal and exile, Patassé's attention had moved on, by which time he had identified new and even more pervasive threats: primarily that presented by the FACA chief of staff, General François Bozizé.

Once again there was no lack of plausibility here. Bozizé had demonstrated ambition, and military coups, after all, have always been, and remain, a highly pervasive malady in Africa. The military high command in any region of such manifest political instability as the Central African Republic can always fairly be suspected of having an unhealthy interest in power.

In many ways Bozizé was an obvious candidate for this. His public persona presented him as a rather slow-witted, avuncular and pedestrian man, disadvantaged in his personal appearance and guttural in speech and yet intellectual, deeply religious and staunchly loyal to his men. According to at least one biographical account, he "... could often be seen chugging around Bangui in a battered car waving to people he knew".[33]

François Bozizé was born in Gabon in 1946, where his father, originally from the Bossangoa region of the Central African Republic, served as a policeman. He was enrolled at the French-run school for military officers in Boar where he distinguished himself early, achieving the rank of captain before the age of thirty. He was later fast-tracked to the rank brigadier-general by Bokassa himself, apparently because he soundly beat a Frenchman who had insulted the emperor. After Bokassa's overthrow in 1979, Bozizé was named defence minister and then minister of information and culture under Kolingba.

In the aftermath of Ange-Félix Patassé's attempt to overthrow Kolingba in 1982, Bozizé fled the county along with Patassé himself, seeking exile in Togo where he and Patassé were said to have developed a personal friendship. In 1989 Bozizé was arrested in Benin and extradited to the CAR where he was detained and subjected to extremely brutal treatment at the hands of state security agents, described by the BBC as 'grotesque torture".[34] He was, however, tried and acquitted in 1991. He then ran against Kolingba in the presidential election that ended Kolingba's rule but lost to Ange-Félix Patassé. He was named army chief of staff by Patassé in 1996, in which capacity he was instrumental in defending the government during the series of army mutinies described in the previous chapter.

However, once again, Patassé's situation, and frame of mind, was such that there were neither friends nor enemies to consider, simply the existence of opportunity and a plethora of opportunists. Patassé was surrounded by wolves and when defending his fore he was simply inviting attack from the rear; in this regard General François Bozizé could hardly have been a better typecast.

Patassé suspected Bozizé because of his current position and his past political activity, but also because Bozizé was a member of the Gbaya ethnic group, the largest in the country, and one that over-spilled the region into neighbouring countries. This naturally allowed Bozizé to cast the ethnic net very widely indeed, and at the core of much of the subterranean political activity in the territory lay the deep undercurrents of tribalism and ethnicity. Bozizé was also, as we have heard, a religious man, and was co-founder of a local evangelical church, *Le Christianisme Céleste Nouvelle Jérusalem*, suspected by Patassé, not unjustifiably, as being a hub of subversive political activity.

In early October 2001, Patassé gave notice of his intention to move against Bozizé by banning *Le Christianisme Céleste Nouvelle Jérusalem* and a week later dismissing him from his position as army chief of staff. The effect of this was to polarize the army. Those loyal to Bozizé remained with him, forming in effect a private militia which immediately assumed the structure of a rebel group. Then, in early November, Patassé authorized the arrest of Bozize, who by then had taken refuge with about a hundred of his loyal supporters—mainly officers of his Gbaya ethnic group—in the barracks of the Territorial Infantry Battalion (BIT), adjoining his residence in the northern suburbs of Bangui.

An amnesty of sorts was negotiated on Bozizé's behalf by General Lamine Cissé, the Senegalese officer in charge of BONUCA. Obviously the existence of two armed camps within the army presaged an escalation in tension, and being at the head of little more than a goodwill mission, General Cissé had every reason to try and cool the political temperature.

Patassé, however, tried once again to arrest Bozizé, ordering an attack on the barracks of the Territorial Infantry Battalion on 3 November, succeeding after five days of fighting, and with the assistance of Libyan troops, in capturing the barracks. Bozize, however, had escaped, fleeing north toward Chad with some 300 loyal troops, reaching the frontier the following day. There he remained for some time, before making his way into temporary exile in France.

In the meanwhile, the attack against the army barracks and attempts by Patassé to arrest Bozizé catalyzed a renewed bout of insecurity in the troubled north of the country, as rebels loyal to Bozizé continued to fight—launching raids from within Chadian territory—and while local rebel-bandits and Chadian commando units ranged the region in pursuit of booty and a vague, quasi-ethnic/political agenda.

From Paris an ebullient and vocal Bozizé claimed the birth of an organized, but as yet unnamed rebel movement. In the meanwhile, and with Bozizé in effect now launching military operations out of Chad, Patassé began fulminating against President Idriss Déby who he accused of backing the rebels in order to destabilize the region as a means to seize control of its projected oil reserves. Needless to say Déby denied these accusations, after which a furious war of words erupted between N'Djamena and Bangui.

The French, meanwhile, now found themselves host to yet another awkward émigré from the Central African Republic. Bozizé, by his own admission, had the presidency in mind and made no secret of the fact that an armed insurrection was his preferred method of achieving it.

Patassé responded with a plea for help from the regional Community of Sahel Saharan States, or CEN-SAD, which, of course, could be seen as little less than an open invitation to Libya. Soon after a CEN-SAD force, consisting of some 300 troops, was deployed to the CAR with the limited mandate of securing the capital. In October of that year this rather ad-hoc force was replaced by a more acceptable regional peacekeeping force, the *Forces Multinationales de la CEMAC*, or FOMUC, provided by the

Central African Economic and Monetary Union, or CEMAC, comprising similar troop demographics to that provided for by CEN-SAD. In addition there were present in the country an indeterminate number of combatants belonging to Congolese Jean-Pierre Bemba's rebel militia, the *Mouvement pour la Libération du Congo,* or MLC.

However, three weeks later, on 25 October 2002, and to mark the first anniversary of Bozizé's exile, supporters of the rebel leader staged a lightning raid on the capital. This attack was beaten back only in extremis, and was successful only thanks to the active involvement of Libyan troops and several hundred members of the MLC.

Bozizé had in the meanwhile slipped his intelligence services surveillance detail in Paris and succeeded in crossing the border into Belgium. From there he was expected to try and make his way to Chad, after which it could be assumed that he would join his men in the field. An urgent petition was directed to Idriss Déby by President Jacques Chirac's adviser on Africa, Michel de Bonnecorse, to expel Bozizé the moment that his presence was detected in the country. Shortly after, Bozizé was indeed intercepted and placed on an aircraft back to Paris.

The French, through the agency of Algerian president, Abdelaziz Bouteflika, then urged Colonel Gaddafi to repatriate his troops from Bangui and to withdraw the two Libyan Marchetti aircraft that had been used to bomb rebel positions in the northern suburbs of Bangui. Thereafter de Bonnecorse lobbied intensively among France's regional allies, principally Chad, the two Congos and Gabon, to consider a joint plan to avoid further bloodshed, and no doubt to deflect any local pressure for direct French involvement by forcing Patassé to negotiate with Bozizé, and if possible to orchestrate a regime change in favour of the latter.

Clearly the walls were beginning to close in on Patassé. Combined French and regional pressure informed him in no uncertain terms that his time had come. As the exiled opposition formed up behind Bozizé, Patassé, distrustful of FOMUC with its elements drawn from Chad, Gabon and Congo, lobbied hard for direct French military assistance. If he was to engage in internal rapprochement, he beseeched, then he was owed by the French some sort of personal security. "There are French soldiers in Côte d'Ivoire," he pleaded, "... why not in the CAR? It's discrimination. I am asking France to send us soldiers."[35]

The French were unmoved, and in an apparent fit of pique, Patassé launched a military campaign with the help of Pierre Bemba's MLC to reclaim the north. His troops managed to seize and occupy the town of Bossangoa in the northeast of the country, after which he convinced himself that his position was sufficiently secure to exclude Bozizé from the pending national debate.

This immediately nullified the exercise and rendered an armed rebellion the only meaningful alternative. The authorities in Paris took a step back, Bozizé was permitted to leave, and shortly afterward he reappeared in N'Djamena. President Idriss Déby made available his 'Force 4' Presidential Guard while Joseph Kabilia, the young president of the Democratic Republic of Congo, supplied the necessary hardware. President Denis Sassou Nguesso provided funds to the tune of 4.6 million euros while moral gravitas was given by the approval of Gabon's Omar Bongo.

Upon this Bozizé marched into Bangui more or less unopposed. FOMUC had been ordered not to interfere and the armed forces did nothing. Bozizé's force comprised only a handful of CAR officers, the most senior of whom was a captain. The remainder of the force was made up of Chadian troops provided by Déby, casting some doubt over the claim that this was a popular movement, but it hardly mattered. On 15 March, 2003 two rebel columns met to seize the capital, meeting no serious resistance, Patassé himself having left the country to participate in a CEN-SAD summit meeting in Niger.

Patassé took temporary refuge in Cameroon and then in Togo. France, meanwhile, refused his repeated requests to apply the standing defence agreement that existed between the two republics. Three hundred French soldiers were nonetheless sent to Bangui for the purpose of protecting French nationals. This was to be the beginning of Opération *Boali.*

CHAPTER NINE:
OPERATION *BOALI*

The French return to the Central African Republic was undertaken under very different rules of engagement. The official literature surrounding Operation *Boali* is rich with the language of support, cooperation and capacity building. However the street urchins of Bangui who saw much and said no less, recognized the naked king and shouted *"Cudali!"* or "Barracuda!" whenever a French patrol came within view.

After four years the French were back; it remained to be seen whether the lofty guarantees of facilitating peace and security once and for all could be maintained.

This was also very much the mood that François Bozizé attempted to project as he mounted the podium and presented himself to the nation for the first time. Despite the obvious anomaly of almost complete outside support, he offered up this change of regime as a popular revolution, promising that in its wake would follow a national recovery programme and broad political inclusion.

However, against this promise of national catharsis, smoke was once again rising over the capital as the liberators, in this case dominated by Chadians, comprehensively looted the

Operation *Boali*: patrolling in Bangui's combat zone.
Source: Ministère de la Défense

Central African Economic and Monetary Union, or CEMAC.
Source: Wikicommons

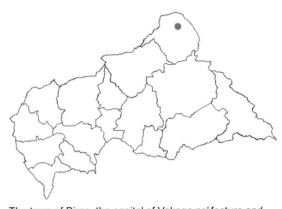

The town of Birao, the capital of Vakaga préfecture and the most northerly administrative centre in the republic.
Source: Wikicommons

capital. Vehicles were commandeered and driven north, packed to the gunwales with booty. Bozizé appeared to do nothing. In fact his hands were tied. He was dependent on the Chadian force and could do nothing to limit the excesses. In fact, as a popular backlash within Bangui began to make itself felt, he was compelled to appeal once again to Idriss Déby for reinforcements, which came in the form of a further 500 Chadian soldiers who maintained the peace while their compatriots removed everything of value from under the noses of the citizens. One hundred and fifty of these men were in due course integrated into FOMUC, which was reinforced and its mandate renewed on 3 June 2003.[36] It was in support of this force, and rhetorically at least, in support of the *Forces Armées Centrafricaines* (FACA), that the French were in the country.

Bozizé, in the meanwhile, suffered from an immediate lack of political legitimacy thanks to his over-dependence on outside security support. This changed in May 2005 with Bozizé's apparently transparent victory at the polls which established him as President of the Republic with few convincing voices of dissent.

Chadian military predominance prevailed, however, illustrated most notably by the fact that the personal bodyguard that surrounded the new president's residence, and accompanied him on all official excursions, comprised eighty Chadian military personnel drawn from President Déby's own ethnic group, the Zaghawas.

The obvious rationale to this was for Bozizé to surround himself with fighting men loyal to an outside president and un-influenced by the ebbs and flows of local ethnic politics.

In the meanwhile, the new president, in whom such hope both internally and externally had been invested, very quickly began to slide into the well-worn channel of corruption, nepotism and ethnic favouritism. He once again sought to concentrate power at the centre while sidelining ethnically-suspect cabinet ministers and technocrats, all of which tended to assure, despite all the early promise, a depressing repetition of the past. It therefore came as a surprise to none when, only a few weeks after Bozizé's assumption of the presidency had been legitimized at the polls, the first signs of renewed armed rebellion began to emerge in the northwest of the country, and in particular surrounding the traditional stronghold of former president Ange-Félix Patassé.

The insecurity in the north of the republic was made up of a complex mixture of local banditry, politically inspired rebellion and simple military indiscipline. Banditry on purely criminal lines was perpetrated largely by a heterogeneous association known as *coupeurs de routes*, or highwaymen, sometimes referred to as *zaraguina*, who were, and remain, criminal gangs involved in kidnap for ransom, looting and general criminality focused along the main transit routes of the region.

Formed initially as an ad hoc civil protection force against this threat, the People's Army for the Restoration of Democracy or, more accurately the *Armée Populaire pour la Restauration de la Démocratie* (APRD), began to take shape, but quickly developed a political agenda and a central political organization that projected its mandate as follows:

The APRD was formed in 2006 following the 2003 coup which overthrew President Ange-Félix Patassé. It is one of several groups which fought in the 2004–2007 Central African Republic Bush War. Initially claiming it wished

Patrolling the streets of Birao. *Source: Wikicommons*

An AML-90 monitors a ferry crossing. *Source: Yves Debay*

A Mirage F1 CR and Transall C-160 at M'poko airport in Bangui. *Source: Yves Debay*

to overthrow current CAR President François Bozizé, the APRD was the last of the three rebel coalitions to engage in the 2007 peace process. The group participated in the 2008 Inclusive Peace Dialog, and in early 2009 entered a coalition government with Bozizé and other civil and military oppositions groups.[37]

The APRD was originally formed from a core of the deposed elements of Patassé's presidential guard, removed for the usual reasons of ethnic incompatibility, and left thereafter to their own devices. Added to this were elements of the former '*libérateurs*' who operated without any defined political agenda and were composed frequently of rogue combatants of Chadian origin. External factors also had a bearing on the volatile situation in the north. The unfolding crisis in Darfur, for example, which complicated matters in the ongoing Chadian crisis, also tended to play a part in the complex web of rebellion and counter-rebellion beginning to take root in the Central African Republic.

However, French hopes to overhaul and professionalize the FACA, and transform it into the professional and apolitical force it had thus far never been, were encouraged somewhat in July 2004, when a deployment of some 200 French-trained FACA troops registered some success in combating the banditry and general insecurity in the north. This kind of encouragement was manna to anxious French policy planners in the Quai d'Orsay. A year after the Bozizé coup a high-ranking foreign office official, Vice-Admiral Giraud, visited Bangui to hand over forty-six vehicles and other general equipment worth over US$3.2 million. Moreover, it was announced that military trainers and support for the CEMAC troops under Operation *Boali* would stay on, meaning in effect that about 200–300 French troops would remain on semi-permanent detachment in the country.

Throughout 2005, however, the number of attacks reported in the north of the country increased steadily. In August contacts took place between government forces, supported directly by the Chadian army, and somewhat less directly by the French, with rebels believed to be members of another uniquely misnamed rebel movement, the FDPC, or *Forces pour la Démocratie du Peuple Centrafricain*. This group was led by a certain Abdoulaye Miskine and was politically aligned to the exiled Patassé. In common with most similar organizations, and in contrast to its lofty nomenclature, the victims of this organization were principally civilian and the objective of the attacks either ethnic in tone or in reprisal for cooperation with the enemy, in this case the FACA, who were themselves not above similar reprisals for the same sorts of reasons.

The APRD, meanwhile, ridiculed somewhat by the central authorities as a *groupuscule complètement folklorique*, or a rustic village militia, claimed responsibility for attacks against the settlements of Marcounda and Kabo in December, and made known its intention to overthrow the Bozizé regime. And so matters continued, until on 30/31 October 2006 rebels of arguably the best organized group, the *Union des Forces Démocratiques pour le Rassemblement*,

French Defence Minister Michèle Alliot-Marie.
Source: Wikicommons

or UFDR, launched an substantive attack against the town of Birao, the capital of Vakaga prefecture and the most northerly administrative centre in the republic.

This was by far the most important regional settlement, with a population of some 14,000, along with whom were captured an arsenal of arms and ammunition, including nine vehicles, among which were two trucks mounted with 14.5mm machine guns that had been abandoned by the FACA. Soon after, the UFDR also seized control of the towns of Ouanda Djallé and Sam Ouandja, even briefly occupying Ndélé, the administrative centre of the neighbouring prefecture of Bamingi-Bangoran, and pressing forward a third prefecture, that of Haute-Kotto in southeast Vakaga.

This dramatic advance and seizure of territory marked a significant and dangerous escalation of hostilities in the north, and an immediate appeal for assistance was made by the government to the international community and to France in particular under a general plea to "... friendly nations, in particular those linked by specific treaties, particularly France, to work for the restoration of the territorial integrity".[38]

Press reports at the time speculated that the incident was a spill-over of the violence and insecurity rampant in Darfur. In fact the boundaries of conflict in the region, be they geographic, ideological or criminal, were impossible to isolate in a region of overlapping and interlocking ethnic conflict. Bozizé nonetheless demanded an explanation from Khartoum, while behind the scenes the necessary diplomatic procedures were under way between Bangui and Paris to allow the French to once again involve themselves in the crisis in the CAR. In the meanwhile, a UFDR spokesman, Captain Abakar Sabone, accused Bozizé of "holding the country hostage" and demanded they start talks about power sharing.[39]

This time, however, the French were available when summoned. Nine years after the closure of her two military bases in the CAR, France was back in the thick of the action.

The raw facts of the ensuring operation are simple. The FACA, with the French offering tactical and logistical support, launched a counter-offensive against the hostile factions on 27 November 2006. Rebel advances were rolled back reasonably effectively in a campaign that lasted no more than a few days. And in a visible sign that the French had no real faith in the independent capacity of the FACA, an Operational Assistance Detachment of eighteen men, including a doctor and two nurses, was deployed to Birao. Three hundred French troops had been involved in the operation while a further hundred were flown into Bangui from other regional bases.

A jeep radio operator during the operation in Kolwezi in 1978.
Source: Wikicommons

Mortars of the 2nd REP in action during a search operation after the capture of the town of Kolwezi. *Source: Wikicommons*

In the meantime, a bloodier battle was fought on the Quai d'Orsay as the French foreign office beat off hostile press questioning over the perennial matter of French intervention in Africa. Word was seeping out that a great deal of gratuitous violence and destruction had accompanied the assault which contrasted steeply with the verbiage of French foreign policy as it had evolved since the last time French troops fired shots in anger in the Central African Republic.

"These are operations that are being led by the CAR army," Defence Minister Michèle Alliot-Marie told Associated Press in Paris, with her tongue no doubt lodged firmly in her cheek. "We have only been supporting them."[40]

Indeed, if this was so it was very close support indeed and as events unfolded, it would grow closer still. On the evening of Sunday, 3 March 2007 UFDR rebels launched a second attack against Birao. French Operational Assistance Detachment personnel commented later that this was a significantly more coordinated and determinate action than anything seen hitherto. "The guys in front of us wanted the skin [sic]," observed one French soldier during a later press interview. "They were equipped with small arms—assault rifles, RPG launchers—and were capable of coordinated action, deploying in pick-up trucks and communicating via satellite phones."[41]

The situation, when it was reported, was deemed sufficiently serious that a Mirage F-1CR fighter was scrambled from N'Djamena to annihilate a 30mm cannon, four pick-ups and a haulage truck belonging to the insurgents. This action was authorized for the immediate defence of the Operational Assistance Detachment that stood the risk of being either annihilated, captured or taken hostage. However, after this initial air assault, the French personnel on the ground remained under

siege; in the midst of a French presidential election at home, a major French airborne operation was quickly authorized, the first in Africa since the iconic 1978 drop by French paras that launched the Battle of Kolwezi.[3]

On the evening of Sunday 4 March 2007, a day after the full moon, ten French paratroops of the 3rd Parachute Regiment (3e RPIMa) tumbled out of a military Transall C-160 in a HALO, or high-altitude-low-opening, jump over Birao with the task of making contact with the isolated Operational Assistance Detachment. The following evening a second, more substantial (HALO) jump was successfully made by a further fifty-eight paratroopers. These landed safely on the Birao landing strip, situated about ten kilometres from the town centre, and that had been surrounded but not defended by the UFDR. Once the landing area had been cleared and secured, Transalls launched from N'Djamena and carrying a company of 3e RPIMa were able to land on the gravel strip, with 130 men going into action as soon as they deplaned.

The operation was brief and dramatic. Birao was retaken and the surrounding area secured. The human cost was no recorded losses on the French side, six FACA dead and eighteen wounded and an unknown number (probably about 30) rebels killed. The operation had been a dramatic success and a vindication of the French rapid reaction policy that complied implicitly with the proviso that such operations be undertaken only with the objective of protecting or securing the freedom of French nationals.

---

[3] The Battle of Kolwezi was a May 1978 airborne operation launched by the French army in Zaire during the Shaba II invasion of that country by the Front for the National Liberation of the Congo. Its objective was to rescue European and Zairian hostages held by Katangese rebels after they overran the city of Kolwezi. The hostages were freed with only light military casualties sustained. The operation was deemed a success.

An REP patrol. *Source: Yves Debay*

A VLRA with its 20mm cannon monitors the road along the Oubangui river. *Source: Yves Debay*

RECAMP was intended to improve interoperability and foster improved relations between the United States, Europe and Central Africa. *Source: Wikicommons*

US and French soldiers inspect a Red Cross clinic being restored as part of the international exercise RECAMP. *Source: Wikicommons*

later with unease as the public ruminated on the reappearance of French interventionism in Africa.

The Élyseé reminded the world of the defence accords linking the country with many of its erstwhile colonial charges and, like it or hate it, these were all legal, limited by terms that had been fully complied with throughout the operation. The soldiers shrugged, as soldiers do, and returned to their bases after a job well done.

It had been generally supposed that it was the FACA that had surrendered itself to the general looting, destruction and violence that took place in the aftermath of the operation, not the French. The French were culpable, if anything, of allowing it to happen. However, comments later recorded by French soldiers present during the operation describe the more likely scenario of rebel elements burning houses as they withdrew from the city, followed by additional destruction wrought by villagers on the homesteads and property of members of the ethnic group, described as the *Goulha*, who had been perceived to be close to the rebels. This represents an eminently plausible explanation under the circumstances and is clearly closer to the truth than the popular myth that French soldiers ran riot in the town, burning, looting and generally acting at complete variance with the traditions of a highly motivated, professional and disciplined force.

France's Opération *Boali*, in the meanwhile, had all the appearance about it that it was in for the long haul. The operation was officially launched on 16 March 2003, but in fact had put boots on the ground as early as October 2002, in support of the 300 or so troops of FOMUC, the first multinational force in the country sponsored and underwritten by the Economic and Monetary Community of Central Africa (CEMAC).

This was one of the first visible manifestations of the new French policy of RECAMP, or African Capacity Building for Peacekeeping, *Capacités Africaines de Maintien de la Paix*. It operated under a strictly limited mandate, described officially as working alongside FACA and FOMUC for the preservation of internal peace by the provision of personnel, logistical support and training. It was based at the French M'poko camp associated with the main airport, which obviously came under its remit, and had a visible presence in Bangui within a radius of some 200 kilometres. The force strength of *Boali* hovered around 200 individuals, including

The diplomatic battle was lost, however, and quite convincingly so. The clinical success of the operation, and the news that no French lives had been lost or injuries sustained, seemed misplaced amid the furrowed brows and humanitarian concern that reverberated throughout French and international civil society. A fortnight or so after the assault, the humanitarian coordinator of the UN in Bangui, Toby Lanzer, led a delegation to Birao, and forgetting perhaps the practicalities of war and indeed the magnified difficulties and horrors that war in Africa seemed to present, wandered glumly through the ruins of the town, drawing comparisons to the recent Russian annihilation of Grozny, and questioning why so much of the settlement had been put to the torch, and why so few evacuees had returned.

Following this, a report by *Human Rights Watch* accused French soldiers of looking on while state security organs committed severe human rights violations. Christophe Gazam Betty, a former CAR ambassador to Paris, now self-declared coordinator of a number of rebel groups, went a step further in a media interview on 20 April, accusing France of committing crimes against humanity by indiscriminately bombing villages in the north of the CAR, suggesting that these actions would be better dealt with by the International Criminal Court. The press in general greeted the news first with some pique at a weeklong news blackout, but

A Mirage F1 CR preperaes for take-off at M'poko. *Source: Yves Debay*

This Jaguar at M'poko did not participate in Operation *Almandin* in 1997 but saw action in 1994's Operation *Turquoise* in Rwanda. Bangui International Airport was a perfect platform from which to to operate in central Africa. From here, in 1983/84, several air raids were launched against Gadaffi forces in northern Chad. *Source: Yves Debay*

an infantry company, maintenance, administration, health, military police personnel, and a small detachment of civilian gendarmerie for the purpose of training and monitoring the local police force.

This limited force, whatever the language of friendly entente that described it, represented an advanced force of military personnel, more or less in direct possession of the main airport, that was in a position to secure the ground for the rapid deployment of a more muscular force that could be deployed directly from France or from any of the regional bases. These were most immediately N'Djamena in Chad, but also from the French forces in Gabon (FFG), where some 1,000 men were based (from among whom had been selected reinforcements for the permanent staff of Opération *Boali* during the airborne assault on Birao).

In the aftermath of the operation, *Boali* was awarded command by a full colonel (replacing a lieutenant-colonel) at the head of the reinforced detachment, 200 of which remained on normal duties associated with the operation, while 150 combat troops remained behind to keep an eye on things in Birao as well as the surrounding region.

A brief note here, in respect of the enemy that had prompted all this, reveals the *Union des Forces Démocratiques pour le Rassemblement* as being a cut above the average in terms of local rebel organizations. The group was a coalition of three separate armed organizations that merged in September 2006: the *Mouvement des Libérateurs Centrafricains pour la Justice* (MLJC) led by Captain Abakar Sabone, the *Groupe d'Action Patriotique pour la Libération de Centrafrique* (GAPLC) led by Michel Djotodia and finally the *Front Démocratique Centrafricain* (FDC) led by Major Hassan Justin, an ex member of Patassé's Presidential Guard.

It was realized in Bangui in the aftermath of the incident that UFDR, reported at that time, or at least accused of being, supported by and allied to Khartoum, that this was an organization that needed to be taken seriously. Likewise the UFDR realized that with the French back in the picture the direction of peace enforcement in the region was liable to be taken more seriously. Thus, On 13 April 2007, a peace agreement was signed between the UFDR and the government that provided for an amnesty for the UFDR, its recognition as a political party, and the eventual integration of its fighters into the army.

CHAPTER TEN:
EUFOR CHAD / CAR

Despite Bozizé's seizing power in a coup, he successfully fought a presidential election in 2005 after two years as a transitional leader, winning a five-year term against an opposition ticket that included both Ange-Félix Patassé and erstwhile defence minister and political ideologue Jean-Jacques Démafouth. Bozizé, however, was still fundamentally reliant on Chad as a buttress for his regime and indeed for his personal security in an environment of growing lawlessness and insecurity.

The northern préfecture of Vakaga, the capital of which is Birao, is bordered on two sides, by Chad to the west and Sudan to the east. It lies sufficiently near the troubled region of Darfur, and sufficiently remote from the administrative centre of Bangui, to be drawn into the vortex of violence and insecurity occasioned by the conflict in Darfur, and complicated by the ongoing enmity and low-level conflcit between Khartoum and N'Djamena.

Bozizé was allied to Chad and therefore alienated from Sudan, and could fairly guess, and made no secret of, his suspicion, that the insecurity in the northern Central African Republic was attributable directly to the Sudanese support of the various hostile armed groups.

The Central African Republic could bring to bear a minimum of weight in any aspect of the multifaceted conflict north of her border, being politically and militarily weakened to the point of almost non-existence. However, for Bozizé to have any hope of bringing an end to the ongoing violence in the region as it affected the CAR, it was necessary for him to attempt some sort of rapprochement with Khartoum, an extremely delicate diplomatic

objective bearing in mind the degree to which he owed his political existence to the support of Chad.

The various generations of conflict in southern Sudan had begun to impact the north of the Central African Republic long before the explosion of violence that in 2003 brought the remote region of Darfur to global attention. Thanks to the geographic delineation of the northern frontier of the Central African Republic, the prefecture of Vakaga could hardly have been better positioned as a staging ground for armed groups involved in the regional conflicts that date back to 1983, and the beginning of the north/south Sudanese civil war. Thousands of Sudan People's Liberation Army (SPLA) fighters sought refuge, food and safe haven in the territory, while at the same time the region was used periodically as a base for attacks launched by the Sudanese armed forces against SPLA positions in the western Bahr el-Ghazal.

Violence of this nature was naturally accompanied by large numbers of refugees, and with these, inevitably, came weaponry and the resultant lawlessness and instability. The signing of the Comprehensive Peace Agreement in January 2005 between the main warring parties in Sudan eased matters somewhat, but by April 2006 the movement of Darfur-based Chadian rebels through northeastern Central African Republic en route to launch attacks against the Chadian capital N'Djamena again heightened tensions in the region.

Bozizé responded to all this with the rather impotent gesture of closing the border between Central African Republic and Sudan, which did nothing to stop the movement of foreign arms and armed combatants through CAR territory. Indeed, in April 2006 an Antonov cargo aircraft either owned by or affiliated with Sudan made two return trips from somewhere in Sudan to Tiroungoulou, a town situated just south of Birao, where a large quantity of military equipment and approximately fifty armed men were unloaded. These were promptly dispersed into the surrounding area. Units of the FACA deployed in the region were powerless, and possibly disinclined, to do anything but observe.

At the end of June, meanwhile, FACA units, supported by FOMUC peacekeepers, were deployed to the area where clashes with armed men in nearby Gordil were reported, contacts that generated an estimated thirty casualties. The rebels allegedly sought to appropriate fuel and other supplies, but did not make known any particular political objectives. By the end of 2006, after Birao had been retaken by the French for the first time, Bozizé had made arrangements to meet with Sudanese president Omar al-Bashir, and indeed al-Bashir had sent an aircraft to Bangui to collect him. At the last minute, however, Bozize was forced to abort the trip after President Déby threatened to withdraw his bodyguard and the Chadian contingent serving in FOMUC. France also, for what it was worth, let Bozizé know that such diplomatic adventures would not win French approval.

However, and despite the regular transit of foreign guerrilla and national forces back and forth through the Central African Republic territory, it has never been proved, or ever realistically asserted, that the Sudan had any particular interest in destabilizing the Central African Republic. The insecurity in the Central African Republic remained a phenomenon related more to banditry, the internal political see-saw and the revolving carousel of ethnic ascendency and decline.

This general regional insecurity, and in particular the Chadian rebel assault launched against the capital in April 2006, known as the Battle of N'Djamena, prompted the deployment of a European Union Force security force, codenamed EUFOR, and based on the United Nations Security Council resolution 1778 of September 2007, the same resolution that authorized the deployment of a mixed UN peacekeeping operation MINURCAT.

The deployment of the European operation was approved by the Council of the European Union on 15 October 2007. The force was mandated to improve the security in eastern Chad and the northeast of the Central African Republic, specifically to provide security for United Nations relief operations and the delivery of humanitarian aid. In many respects it was a bridging operation prior to the deployment of the MINURCAT mission that would follow later.

It was the French, as might be expected, who were the primary force behind the deployment, and they who contributed the lion's share of troops, equipment and logistical support. The launch of the operation was somewhat fated from the onset, with numerous delays experienced in generating troops and equipment, including the all important helicopters, which was seen by many as symptomatic of a noticeable reluctance on the part of EU members other than France to throw their weight behind an operation that few trusted and even fewer wanted to be part of. Outweighing

Sudanese President Omar al-Bashir. *Source: Wikicommons*

French President Nicolas Sarkozy. *Source: Wikicommons*

this, however, was a similar reluctance to stand up to the French or risk embarrassing the newly elected French president, Nicolas Sarkozy. Indeed, the deadlock was only resolved when France contributed a further 500 men and ten helicopters.

Further delays occurred when three Chadian rebel groups launched an offensive against the government of President Déby early in 2008, reaching the outskirts of the capital N'Djamena before being driven back by the Chadian army and Darfurian rebels allied with Déby, both no doubt enjoying support from the French. In a statement issued on 4 February, the United Nations Security Council strongly condemned the attacks, tending to support the French position, with the French themselves making no secret of the fact that they were perfectly willing to intervene militarily in support of Déby if push came to shove.

The mission began its deployment in February, reaching its operational limit on 15 March 2008. The EU operational commander was Lieutenant-General Patrick Nash of the Irish Defence Force, although, with a French contingent of 2,500 personnel out of a total of 3,700, French and EU force commander Brigadier-General Jean-Philippe Ganascia carried equal if not greater weight.

Other contributing nations included the spectrum of the European Union members, with the exception of the United Kingdom and Germany (Germany sent just four soldiers to the operational headquarters, with none in the field), notable absentees it might be surmised, hinting at an overall lack of consensus surrounding the operation.

On the whole the mission attracted very little positive reportage, with the exception perhaps of the airy and institutionalized optimism of the United Nations itself. It could not, therefore, be reasonably claimed that the deployment was a success. Certainly the operational and logistical, and indeed perhaps more importantly, the geographic difficulties, rendered much of what was attempted symbolic, expensive and irrelevant.

The only aggressive action fought through the operation was by the French. On 4 March 2008 two French special forces soldiers driving a soft-skinned vehicle strayed a short distance into Sudan from Chad, and were fired upon by Sudanese forces. One of the soldiers was killed and reported missing while the other was wounded. French soldiers then entered Sudan to search for the

EUFOR peacekeeping force in Chad.
Source: Ministerstvo obrany České republiky

EUFOR.
Source: Ministerstvo obrany České republiky

missing soldier. They came under fire and fired back, killing a Sudanese soldier. The missing soldier's body was found by the Sudanese army on 5 March and was taken to Khartoum to be turned over to the French. However, one of the soldier's grenades detonated as his body was being removed, killing four Sudanese workers.

The death was also recorded of Warrant Officer Gilles Polin, a paratrooper of 1st RPIMa who was killed in an ambush by rebels in the tri-border area on 5 March 2008. Two foreign legionnaires of the 2nd Battalion based at their Camp des Etoiles military base in the city of Abeche were killed by a fellow legionnaire of Brazilian origin who, in an apparent fit of depression, shot dead his comrades, a Togolese peacekeeper and a Chadian civilian from whom he stole a horse, before he headed off unaided into the desert.

The killings sparked a brief manhunt involving helicopters and troops from EUFOR and MINURCAT before the rogue soldier was found exhausted a few kilometres east of Abeche.

In the meanwhile, among the many problems experienced by the EUFOR mission—these included the command and control difficulties inherent in a heterogeneous force of its size, the logistics of deployment in such a remote and under-developed region (the Darfur–Chad–CAR triangle), the limitations imposed by its official mandate and the expectations of local people and such mundane concerns as the use of available water in an environment where water is perhaps the supreme currency—was the perceived partiality of a force dominated by the French. In this regard it is important to remember that a deep history of French military intervention and involvement had already been forged in the region, and indeed the fact that the French had been long-time supporters of President Idriss Déby did not help in the slightest. A great deal of diplomatic effort was employed by General Nash and the EU high representative, Javier Solana, to dispel any suggestion that the EUFOR operation was linked or associated in any way with standing French commitments in the region and in particular the prosecution of the ongoing Opération Épervier in Chad.

Despite this and bearing in mind the obvious fact that both Bozizé in the Central African Republic and Idriss Déby in Chad manoeuvred openly for mandate concessions with a view to using the deployment to support their individual regimes, accusations of impartiality were inevitable. This was particularly the case with the various rebel groups, all of whom saw the EUFOR deployment as configured to maintain incumbent regimes.

Chadian rebels in particular accused EUFOR of partiality toward the Déby regime, threatening to attack the European force if it stood in their way. However, in the event, only minor clashes took place between EUFOR and the rebels, which, in turn angered Déby who began to accuse EUFOR of aiding rebel groups, thereby sparking off a diplomatic row between him, Brussels and EUFOR.

There can be little doubt that the EUFOR operation was in almost every respect a French operation padded by a barely significant and patently political pan-European contingent. Over and above their troop commitments, the French provided the operational headquarters and the bulk of its staff situated at Mont Valerian in the southern France, the force commander who effectively commanded the operation, a 600-man rapid reaction force which, it can be assumed, should any real fighting have taken place, would have been at the centre of it. In terms of logistics, transport, fuel, maintenance, communications and supply, the French provided the lion's share, in terms both of matériel and organization. The French permanent base in Chad was obviously available at all times as part of Opération Épervier to provide aerial reconnaissance and helicopter medevac facilities, plus all the heavy lifting in terms of air cargo, transporting some twelve tonnes daily.

A secondary complication of the EUFOR operation was its existence alongside the United Nations MINURCAT deployment for which it served ostensibly as a bridging operation. On 15 March 2009 EUFOR was officially replaced in the region, with many of the European Union and allied troops simply swapping their berets for blue helmets and essentially continuing as they had prior to this. MINURCAT conformed to the same Security Council authorization as the EUFOR deployment and to a broadly similar mandate. It was, however, a combined, civilian, police and military operation, and:

> ... by that resolution, the Council authorized a

A Mirage F1 CR at M'poko. *Source: Yves Debay*

A Mirage F1 CR from RCA's *Groupe Champagne. Source: Yves Debay*

multidimensional presence intended to help create the security conditions conducive to a voluntary, secure and sustainable return of refugees and displaced persons, inter alia by contributing to the protection of refugees, displaced persons and civilians in danger, by facilitating the provision of humanitarian assistance in eastern Chad and the northeastern CAR and by creating favourable conditions for the reconstruction and economic and social development of those areas.

Events surrounding the work and deployment of MINURCAT fall outside of the scope of this narrative thanks to the fact that it contained no official French contingent members among the military deployments, although the French were represented among the police members included. However, MINURCAT remained operational until 31 December 2010, in accordance with Security Council resolution 1923 (2010), and at the request of the Chadian government, which had pledged full responsibility for protecting civilians on its territory.

CHAPTER ELEVEN:
CONCLUSION

"This suffering of the black man is the suffering of all men.
This open wound in the soul of the black man is
an open wound in the souls of all men"
—President Nicolas Sarkozy
in a speech delivered in Dakar, 26 July 2007

On 23 January 2011 a presidential and parliamentary election was held in the Central African Republic that saw François Bozizé elected to a second term as president. Ange-Félix Patassé died in Douala, Cameroon three months later, aged 74, his passing attributed to complications from diabetes. A year earlier André Kolingba had died at aged 73 while seeking medical treatment in Paris. Jean-Bédel Bokassa, having been tried and sentenced to death in absentia for the murder of political opponents, unexpectedly appeared in the republic in October 1988 after seven years of exile. He was retried in a tribunal that began in December 1986, continuing to June 1987, after which he was found guilty of a variety of crimes, although not that of cannibalism, an accusation that had been made early in his rule and that had stuck with him ever since. He was sentenced to death, but escaped the gallows thanks to Kolingba's apparent dislike of the death penalty which he voided in the case of Bokassa. The ageing leader was released soon after in a general amnesty, dying in 1996 after proclaiming himself the thirteenth apostle and a personal friend of the Pope. On the fiftieth anniversary of independence, the erstwhile emperor was officially rehabilitated.

After a decade in power, Bozizé emerged as a reasonably credible leader by regional standards but, despite that, was unable to reverse the national decline, and the fact that he continued to owe his political existence to French and other international support. A foreign policy journal article published in August 2010 remarked extremely adroitly on the situation in the blighted republic.

The Central African Republic is a black hole of governance at the centre of the continent. Since declaring independence from France in 1960 it has served up a veritable tasting menu of African despotisms: military dictatorships, civilian kleptocracies, and even an 'empire,' complete with an emperor on a golden throne. None lasted much more than a decade before the chef brought out an equally unpalatable new course. Bozizé has fared no better than his predecessors, ruling a territory the size of Texas with a GDP significantly smaller than that of Pine Bluff, Arkansas. As it has for the last two decades, the CAR under Bozizé gets by only through massive quantities of foreign aid, which has familiar corrosive effects on government. As one traveller has written, "Foreign aid is to the CAR what cocaine is to Colombia."[42]

Bozizé may not have fared much better, but he did survive long enough to emerge victorious in two reasonably free and fair presidential elections, which under the circumstances was no small achievement. His methodology in dealing with the ongoing armed rebellions had settled into a pattern not unfamiliar in other parts of Africa. Usually this pattern involved the rebel seizure of one or other of the prefectural capitals, digging in for a day or two, chasing off the poorly equipped and unmotivated FACA garrison, after which Bozizé would dispatch his own soldiers with French support to retake the town. The rebels would duly negotiate and eventually arrive in the capital as Bozizé supporters, their leadership absorbed into government and each lieutenant offered high military rank.

And thus it continued. Inasmuch as it was sustainable, it was exploited. The incumbents grow rich in preparation for exile, after which they fly out to another of the Francophone family with the possibility of returning at a later date as a UN special adviser or a presidential candidate. With a multiplicity of armed factions clamouring for booty and attention, the principle of divide and rule perpetuated itself. The best that could be said of the Central African Republic at the turn of the first millennial decade was that it was encumbered with less malevolent violence than that in Chad and Sudan, and without the spiralling cycle of ethnic violence and insecurity so endemic in the eastern DRC.

All this, of course, is the cynical view. United Nations debates on the mater remain filled with all the lofty prognostications that a man such as Bozizé would wish to hear as a positive indictment

Jean-Pierre Bemba.
Source: Wikicommons

Charles Taylor.
Source: Wikicommons

Thabo Mbeki.
Source: Wikicommons

Lionel Jospin
Source: Wikicommons

of his government, despite the fact that in real terms he represents nothing other than a continuation of past decay and pessimism for the future. However, some optimism within the context of time and place is evident. In November 2010 the trial at the International Criminal Court of ex-Congolese vice-president Jean-Pierre Bemba convened to consider charges accumulated as a consequence of the actions of his MLC rebel group between 2002 and 2003. The lengthy trial of Charles Taylor, the Liberian warlord who set the standard for post-modern violence and misrule in Africa, returned a guilty verdict after years of tortuous hearings.

On 13 April 2007, meanwhile, a peace agreement between the government and the UFDR rebel group was signed, but as Jean-Pierre Bemba sat and listened to the charges against him being read at the Hague, CAR rebels of the fringe Convention of Patriots for Justice and Peace (CPJP) attacked the town of Birao, capital of the Vakaga prefecture, killing four soldiers and capturing and wounding others. The CPJP, incidentally, are the only substantive rebel group remaining outside a broad peace process that has been ongoing since the signing in 2008 of a ceasefire between the government and the main *Union des Forces Démocratiques pour le Rassemblement*.

For the French, the crisis in Darfur projected the troubled region of the Chad/CAR/Sudan triangle into the wider global consciousness and replaced the French military predominance with a panoply of international missions and organizations. Barring the presence of military advisers, by the end of the first decade of the new millennium, no official French military garrison existed in the Central African Republic.

By 2010, *Françafrique* consisted of just five mainland French military bases. These were: 2,000 men stationed in Côte d'Ivoire as part of Operation *Unicorn*, the French armed forces peacekeeping operation in support of the United Nations Operation in Côte d'Ivoire; 2,000 men of the French Forces of Cape Verde (FFCV) stationed in Senegal; 980 French Forces in Gabon (FFG), the oldest permanent base of France in Africa; 2,900 men of the French army, air force and navy stationed in Djibouti; and of course the 1,500 men and various military branches stationed in Chad as a consequence of the ongoing Opération *Épervier*.[43] This deployment is scheduled to wind up soon.

Perhaps the most potent sea change in the new millennium, however, was the election of Nicolas Sarkozy as the centre/right

Former US President George W. Bush and Senegalese President Abdoulaye Wade. *Source: Wikicommons*

president of the Fifth Republic. At 52, Sarkozy is one of the youngest men in recent years to assume the leadership, four years older than Giscard d'Estaing, it is true, but a very different type of man.

Both men could claim aristocratic links, in Sarkozy's case through his father, Pál István Ernő Sárközy de Nagy-Bócsa, a minor Hungarian aristocrat. Sarkozy himself grew up in the middle reaches of Parisian society, abandoned by his father and raised by his Greek/Jewish mother. He was modestly educated and unremarkable in his academic achievements, but later recognized as a natural politician and a man of unusual charisma. He was also acknowledged to possess rare courage in his political decision, supported by unwavering conviction and a willingness to shake off long-established conventions and debunk many of the long-held French traditions of 'politics as usual'.

His approach to Africa and the status of French military involvement on the continent was a case in point. In a landmark speech, made just two months after assuming office, Sarkozy spoke before students, teachers and politicians at the University of Dakar, stating that colonization had been a mistake—which no doubt allowed many in the audience to settle comfortably in their seats in the expectation of a palatable polemic delivered against European imperialism—followed a moment later by the scandalous comment:

The tragedy of Africa is that the African man has never really entered history. The African peasant, who for thousands of years, lives with the seasons, whose ideal of life is to be in harmony with nature, knows only the eternal cycle of time punctuated by the endless repetition of the same gestures and same words. In this imaginary world where everything starts always, there is no place for human adventure nor for the idea of progress.[44]

This set the tone for the remainder of Sarkozy's speech, and after a sharp intake of breath across the black Diaspora, the reaction was forceful, angry and not altogether unpredictable. Many Afrophile commentators sought to remind the French president that human history had commenced in Africa, which was fallacious under the circumstances, and affixing a rather simplistic interpretation on Sarkozy's intended meaning. Senegalese President Abdoulaye Wade, however, was more to the point, and condemned the speech as unacceptable. This it might have been but it was very much in the Sarkozy style and was perhaps delivered as a short, sharp shock in preparation for the later announcement that the military cooperation agreements that had underwritten French involvement in the region for some half a century would shortly be revised, and indeed, renegotiated.

A year later Sarkozy was in South Africa, delivering a somewhat modified version of this speech to the South African Parliament in Cape Town: "Today the old model of relations between France and Africa are no longer understood by new generations of Africans," he said, "and indeed by the French public. We find ourselves in a situation where our political, military and economic engagement alongside Africa is seen by many not as a sincere willingness to help, but as neo-colonial interference; but should we, at the same time, display indifference [toward Africa], we are accused of withdrawing, or a lack of commitment; of abandonment or ingratitude."[45]

All this set the tone for perhaps the most important policy decision that Sarkozy had made in regard to Africa. His belief appeared to be that old notions of cooperation and partnership between France and Africa had run their course. He emphasized many areas of French willingness to pour resources into Africa and to open her metropolitan institutions to Africans, reciprocated by a sense of entitlement that had not been the intended consequence of *Françafrique* as it had been defined by de Gaulle and refined by later generations of French leadership.

To this effect Sarkozy announced what would have little practical impact on South Africa, but which would ramificate deeply throughout Francophone Africa and would redefine the standing relationship that members of that old club, or as Sarkozy seemed to see it, that old kindergarten of Francophone Africa.

South African President Thabo Mbeki had introduced into the global political lexicon the term 'African Renaissance' but he did so somewhat aloof from how the central European powers might interpret this as it related to them.

Sarkozy made reference then to the rebel attacks against the Chadian capital of N'Djamena that had taken place just weeks earlier and stated, not altogether truthfully, that French forces had been restrained from the type of direct military involvement that had become so entrenched in the psyche of both France and Chad in the long history of the conflict. "This change was necessary," he explained, "and the reason is simple. The French military presence in Africa is still grounded in agreements reached in the aftermath of decolonization, 50 years ago."[46] He continued:

I wish in this regard, to make four proposals.

The first deals with defence agreements between France and Africa. These must reflect the Africa today, not the Africa of yesterday. They must be based on the strategic interests of France and its African partners. I'm not saying that we should necessarily scrap and erase everything in one stroke. But I do say that France wishes to initiate discussions with all concerned African states in order to adapt existing agreements to the realities of the present. We would be open to dialogue with all those who wish to establish a new partnership.

Secondly, I propose to recast our relations on the principle of transparency. Transparency is the best guarantee of strong and lasting relationships, and the best antidote to mistakes and misunderstandings that relate to the bonds that unite France and Africa. Contrary to past practice, our agreements will be published in full. I also intend to closely involve the French parliament with the broad guidelines of the policy of France in Africa.

Thirdly, I propose that the French military presence in Africa be configured first and foremost to help Africa build and sustain, as it would like to do, its own system of collective security. The African Union wishes to have standby forces by the year 2010–2012? So do we. France never intended to maintain an indefinite military presence in Africa.

Finally, my last proposal aims to make Europe a major partner in the cause of African peace and security. It is in all our interests, because a strong Europe needs a strong Africa.[47]

All of this was a far cry from the stagnant policy forged by de Gaulle, and tentatively altered by a half century of political succession, but never substantively altered to suit the changing demands of progress. This new policy was defined by Lionel Jospin as neither interference nor indifference. Interestingly, however, the case of Côte d'Ivoire was mentioned frequently as being specifically included in this plan, as if it might be imagined that she would not.

And then, in late 2010, Ivorian elections resulted in a loss to the incumbent, President Laurent Gbagbo, narrowly defeated by opposition candidate Alassane Ouattara. The Independent Electoral Commission confirmed the victory of Ouattara, prompting Gbagbo to appeal to the Constitutional Council which declared the results invalid. Gbagbo refused to vacate his office, quickly taking the presidential oath of office and by that plunging the nation into a political crisis that would end in civil war. After months of unsuccessful negotiations, of plaintive regional diplomacy, threats, entreaty and despair, sporadic violence between the supporters of both parties erupted in open conflict as forces loyal to Ouattara seized control of most of the country. Gbagbo, meanwhile, dug in in Abidjan, the country's largest city, vowing to fight to the death.

On 4 April non-military United Nations personnel began to be evacuated from the capital as heavy fighting began to affect the city centre and the area around the presidential palace, where Gbagbo had retreated and, surrounded by a dwindling force of loyalist soldiers, appeared ready to make a last stand. French troops of the 43rd BIMA (Marine Infantry Battalion), located in Port-Bouet near the airport, were placed on standby as hundreds of French reinforcements began arriving at Abidjan airport.

Soon after, the French, in cooperation with UN forces, went into action. Helicopter attacks were launched against pro-Gbagbo military installations aimed at neutralizing heavy artillery and armoured vehicles. Eyewitnesses reported seeing two French attack helicopters firing missiles at the Akouédo military camp in Abidjan. Several military vehicles belonging to troops loyal to Laurent Gbagbo were destroyed during a helicopter-borne mission to rescue Japan's ambassador, Yoshifumi Okamura, trapped during heavy fighting. The following day, combined UN and French forces carried out further air strikes against Gbagbo's remaining heavy weapons, using the formidable Mil Mi-24 and Aérospatiale Gazelle attack helicopters. The attack inflicted heavy damage to the presidential palace. The palace was stormed and Gbagbo arrested by pro-Quattara forces, bringing the brief but bloody episode to a conclusion. United Nations and French forces justified their involvement as being necessary for the protection of civilians and UN and French forces in the country. About this—and the usual political questions surrounding the truth of it—nothing was unique, however French action in direct support of a frustrated non-incumbent certainly was; all of which left Sarkozy—were he in any way capable of feeling such—embarrassed. The question of a revised French military cooperation policy in Africa seemed to be in tatters.

Within a month Sarkozy was in the Ivorian capital, Yamoussoukro, alongside the now de facto president Alassane Ouattara, pledging his full support and attempting to inject the idea that a French military garrison within the territory still had a role to play.

Obviously Ouattara could hardly disagree. "It is important to be in Côte d'Ivoire along with Alassane Ouattara," Sarkozy crowed for the sake of assembled international press, "... for democracy, for Africa!" And for the sake of the local white French population he added later: "We will keep military forces here to protect our citizens."[48]

And so it was.

In the meanwhile, deep in the interior, the residue of the French military presence in the Central African Republic continued with the ongoing Opération *Boali*, consisting of an operational training detachment (DIO) that comprised six members and an infantry company acting primarily in support of FOMUC. FOMUC, meanwhile, had been rebadged on 12 July 2008 the Central African Multinational Force, or (FOMAC), and in July 2008 rebadged again the Mission for the Consolidation of Peace (MICOPAX). MICOPAX is officially an initiate of the Economic Community of Central African States (ECCAS).

In 2011 Opération *Boali* was made up of 200 troops, based mainly in Bangui, and including a headquarters, the abovementioned infantry company—from July 2010 onward the French 27e Mountain Infantry Battalion (27e BCA) was on secondment to Opération *Boali*—and a detachment of support personnel consisting of maintenance, administration, health and military police. The detachment had no official fighting capability but, as usual, stood to be rapidly reinforced from France or other regional bases.

Under the French *capacités africaines de maintien de la paix* (RECAMP) programme, under which efforts were made to bolster the capacity *armées nationales* to conduct their own national and regional peacekeeping, Opération *Boali* concerned itself with tactical support, and operational support if needed, or the African stabilization force MICOPAX. It also, perhaps more as an exercise in entente than in any real hope of advancement, provides administrative, technical, financial and logistical support, as well as operational training, for units of the *Forces Armées Centrafricaines* (FACA). It also provides operational training of African troops engaged in MICOPAX before their deployment in the field.

Politically, the situation in the Central African Republic remains a continuum. According to a UNDP report issued in 2006, the Central African Republic has taken "a great leap backwards" since the 1970s. According to figures issued by the International Monetary Fund in 2010, the nation languishes at number 178 out of 183 countries in terms of Gross Domestic Product. Sixty-seven per cent of the country lives in poverty, with an income of less than one dollar a day. Life expectancy dipped below 40 in 2005, with the rapid spread of the AIDS pandemic largely to blame, and more than one child in ten dying before the age of five. Less than half of adults are literate while the rate of school attendance fell from sixty-three per cent to forty-three per cent between 1995 and 2000.[49]

The concluding comment of this narrative belongs to Thierry Bingaba, a former minister of economy and finance under General Kolingba, who returned to Bangui in 2007 after a ten-year absence and remarked of his impressions that: "The only change I noticed was that trees have grown along the entire length of the Avenue des Martyrs. Apart from that, I saw building sites that were in the same state they were in ten years ago."[50]

APPENDIX I:
CENTRAL AFRICAN REPUBLIC: MINURCA MANDATE

MINURCA was established by Security Council resolution 1159 (1998) of 27 March 1998 with the following initial mandate:

To assist in maintaining and enhancing security and stability, including freedom of movement, in Bangui and the immediate vicinity of the city;

To assist the national security forces in maintaining law and order and in protecting key installations in Bangui;

To supervise, control storage, and monitor the final disposition of all weapons retrieved in the course of the disarmament exercise;

To ensure security and freedom of movement of United Nations personnel and the safety and security of United Nations property;

To assist in coordination with other international efforts in a short-term police trainers' programme and in other capacity-building efforts of the national police, and to provide advice on the restructuring of the national police and special police forces;

To provide advice and technical support to the national electoral bodies regarding the electoral code and plans for the conduct of the legislative elections.

By its resolution 1182 (1998) of 14 July 1998, the Security Council recognizes that MINURCA, in implementing its mandate:

May conduct limited-duration reconnaissance missions outside Bangui, and other tasks involving the security of United Nations personnel in accordance with paragraph 10 of resolution 1159 (1998).

By its resolution 1201 (1998) of 15 October 1998, the Security Council welcomed the announcement by the authorities in the Central African Republic to hold legislative elections on 22 November and 13 December 1998, and decided that the mandate of MINURCA shall include support for the conduct of legislative elections, and in particular:

The transport of electoral materials and equipment to selected sites and to the sous-préfectures, as well as the transport of United Nations electoral observers to and from electoral sites;

The conduct of a limited but reliable international observation of the first and second rounds of the legislative elections; Ensuring the security of electoral materials and equipment during their transport to and at the selected sites, as well as the security of the international electoral observers.

By its resolution 1230 (1999) of 26 February 1999, the Security Council authorized MINURCA:

To play a supportive role in the conduct of the presidential elections, in conformity with the tasks previously performed during the legislative elections of November/December 1998, recognizing the major responsibility which the United Nations Development Programme would have in the coordination of electoral assistance;

To supervise the destruction of confiscated weapons and ammunition under MINURCA control.

APPENDIX II:
MILITARY AGREEMENTS BETWEEN FRANCE AND AFRICAN COUNTRIES

Defence Agreements	Year of Signature
Cameroon	1974
Central African Republic	1960
Comores	1973
Djibouti	1977
Gabon	1960
Côte d'Ivoire	1961
Senegal	1974
Togo	1963
Military Assistance Agreements	**Year of Signature**
Algeria	1967
Benin	1975
Burkina Faso	1961
Burundi	1969
Cameroon	1974
Central African Republic	1969
Chad	1976
Comores	1978
Congo	1974
Djibouti	1977
Gabon	1960
Libya	1978
Madegascar	1973
Mauritania	1976
Mauritius	1979
Niger	1977
Rwanda	1975
Senegal	1974
Seychelles	1979
Togo	1976
Tunisia	1973
Zaire	1974

APPENDIX III:
FRENCH INTERVENTIONS IN AFRICA

Since independence from its former colonies, France has intervened militarily forty times in Africa by virtue of agreements and defence cooperation or to assist its nationals. Here is a chronology of key interventions.

1961 – Operation *Bulldog* alt: *Long Plough*, undertaken for the maintenance of the naval base at Bizerte, Tunisia.

1964 – Intervention in Gabon to restore the presidency of Leon M'ba to office after a coup perpetrated by a section of the army.

1968–1972 – Operations *Limousin* and *Bison* against a rebellion in Chad's Tibesti province.

1977 – Operation *Verbena* in Zaire, mounted ostensibly by Morocco, with the support of France, in support of Mobutu against a local rebellion in Shaba province.

1978 – Foreign Legion action in the Zairian mining town of Kolwezi to free some 3,000 civilians from capture by the rebel Katanga National Liberation Front of Congo (FLNC).

1978–1980 – Operation *Pout* in Chad against the National Liberation Front of Chad (Frolinat).

1979–1981 – Operation *Barracuda* in Central African Republic to depose Emperor Bokassa and return David Dacko to power.

1983 – Operation *Manta* in support of Chadian President Habré.

1985 – Jaguar fighter jets bomb the Libyan air base of Wadi Dum in northern Chad.

1986 – About 150 French paratroopers arrive as reinforcements in Togo after an attempted coup against President Gnassingbe Eyadema.

1986 – Operation *Épervier* (*Sparrowhawk*) in Chad; 900 troops deployed against Libyan forces.

1989 – Operation *Oside* in the Comoros after the assassination of President Ahmed Abdallah and the takeover of the island republic mercenaries under Bob Denard

1990 – Operation *Shark* in Gabon. Some 2,000 French soldiers evacuate 1,800 foreign nationals and provide support to the regime faced with riots and civil unrest in Libreville and Port Gentil.

1990–1993 – Mission, or Operation *Noroit* in Rwanda in support of President Juvenal Habyarimana against the rebel movement, the Rwandan Patriotic Front.

1991 – 1,000 soldiers sent to Kinshasa after demonstrations against Mobutu.

1992–1994 – Operation *Oryx* in Somalia, then placed under the US command of the mission *Restore Hope*.

1993 – Operation *Lock Wall* in Zaire to evacuate French nationals after riots begun by soldiers in Kinshasa, during which the ambassador of France, Philippe Bernard, was killed.

1994 – Operation *Amaryllis* in Rwanda to evacuate European nationals after the assassination of President Habyarimana and the beginning of the genocide.

1994 – Operation *Turquoise*, involving 2,500 French troops in Zaire and in western Rwanda, officially described as a mission to protect civilians.

1995 – Operation *Azalea* in the Comoros to confront mercenaries under Bob Denard and suppress a coup against President Said Mohamed Djohar.

1996–1997 – Operations *Almandine* I and II, using 2,300 French troops to suppress a series of military mutinies and restore order in Bangui after the murder of two French soldiers.

1997 – Operation *Antelope* in the Congo; evacuation of 6,500 foreigners during fighting Brazzaville.

1996–2007 – Operation *Aramis* in Cameroon in support of the Cameroonian armed forces against Nigeria for control of the Bakassi peninsula.

1998 – Operation *Malachite* in the Democratic Republic of Congo to evacuate foreigners from Kinshasa.

1999 – Operation *Khor Anga* in Djibouti.

2002 – Operation *Unicorn*, a peacekeeping force deployed to Côte d'Ivoire after a rebellion threatening the presidency of President Laurent Gbagbo.

2003 – Operation *Artemis* in Ituri (DRC); France provides the bulk of a contingent deployed by the UN.

2004 – Destruction of aircraft belonging to the Ivorian army after the bombing of Bouaké, in which nine soldiers of the Licorne force were killed; the evacuation of French nationals.

2008 – Protection of the N'Djamena airport and evacuation of French nationals in Chad.

2008 – Logistical support to the Djibouti army; Eritrea.

2011 – Côte d'Ivoire.

NOTES

1   Morehead, Alan, *The White Nile*, Hamish Hamilton, London, 1960, p. 342.

2   Cf. Pierre Saulnier, *Le Centrafrique: Entre Mythe et Réalité*, Paris, 1998, p. 81–96.

3   *Central African Republic: Anatomy of a Phantom State*, Crisis Group Africa Report N° 136, 13 December 2007.

4   Chipman, John, *French Power in Africa*, Blackwell, Oxford, 1989, p. 7.

5   Giradet, quoted: Chipman, John, *French Power in Africa*, Blackwell, Oxford, 1989, p. 75.

6   Andrew, Christopher M. & Kanya-Forstner, A.S. *France Overseas, The Great War and the Climax of French Imperial Expansion*, Thames & Hudson, London, 1981, p. 250.

7   Charles Robert Ageron, quoted: Chipman, John, *French Power in Africa*, Blackwell, Oxford, 1989, p. 76.

8   Arnold, Guy, *Africa: A Modern History*, Atlantic Books, London, 2005, p. 40.

9   Count de Marenches, *The Evil Empire,* Sidgwick & Jackson, 1988, p. 58.

10   Meredith, Martin, *The State of Africa: A History of Fifty Years of Independence*, Jonathan Ball, Cape Town, 2005, p. 225.

11   *Time* Magazine, *Mounting a Golden Throne*, 19 December 1977.

12   Count de Marenches, *The Evil Empire,* Sidgwick & Jackson, 1988, p. 62.

13   Meredith, Martin, *The State of Africa: A History of Fifty Years of Independence*, Jonathan Ball, Cape Town, 2005, p. 230.

14   Count de Marenches, *The Evil Empire,* Sidgwick & Jackson, 1988, p. 64.

15   Count de Marenches, *The Evil Empire,* Sidgwick & Jackson, 1988, p. 65.

16   Count de Marenches, *The Evil Empire,* Sidgwick & Jackson, 1988, p. 67.

17   Count de Marenches, *The Evil Empire,* Sidgwick & Jackson, 1988, p. 67.

18   Quoted in Loubat, *L'Ogre de Berengo*, 13–14.

19   de Almeida, Hermione & Gilpin, George H., *Indian Renaissance: British Romantic Art and the Prospect of India*, Ashgate, Burlinton VT, 2005, p. 294.

20   Griffin, Christopher William, *French Grand Strategy in the Fifth Republic*, Faculty of the Graduate School University of Southern California, May 2009.

21   Chipman, John, *French Power in Africa*, Blackwell, Oxford, 1989, p. 117.

22   Gower, Geoffrey, *African Dances*, Faber, London, 1935, p. 131.

23   *Journal Officiel*, Assembly Nationale, 19 December, – 12323.

24   *Project Socialiste pour la France des Années 80*, Club Socialiste du Livre, Paris, 1980, p. 359.

25   'Le Président Kolingba concède le multipartisme', Reuters, 23 April 1991.

26   *Central African Republic: Anatomy of a Phantom State*, Crisis Group Africa Report N° 136, 13 December 2007.

27   *New York Times* Company, 26 May, 1996.

28   Sams, Katie E. & Berman, Eric G., *Peacekeeping in Africa: Capabilities and Culpabilities*, United Nations Institute for Disarmament Research/Institute for Security Studies, Geneva, 2000, p. 224.

29   Sams, Katie E. & Berman, Eric G., *Peacekeeping in Africa: Capabilities and Culpabilities*, United Nations Institute for Disarmament Research/Institute for Security Studies, Geneva, 2000, p. 227.

30   Sarooshi, Danesh, *The United Nations and the Development of Collective Security: The Delegation by the UN Security Council of Its Chapter VII Powers*, Oxford University Press, Oxford, 2000, p. 246.

31   Lorenz, Joseph P., *Peace, Power, and the United Nations: A Security System for the Twenty-First Century*, Westview Press, Boulder, CO, 1999, p. 89.

32   Prepared for the Internet by the Information Technology Section/ Department of Public Information (DPI); maintained by the Peace and Security Section of DPI in cooperation with the Department of Peacekeeping Operations.

33   *Trickey Erick: notablebiographies.com*

34   Lucy Jones, BBC.

35   'Le président Patassé réclame l'envoi de soldats français', Agence France Presse, 5 February 2002.

36   The United Nations, Security and Peacekeeping in Africa—Lessons and Prospects.

37   Wikipedia Foundation.

38   'La communauté internationale appelée à défendre l'intégrité territoriale de la RCA', Agence Centrafricaine de Presse (ACAP), 31 October 2006.

39   'Central African govt asks France to help repel rebels', Reuters, 31 October 2006.

40   'La France appuie l'armée centrafricaine contre les rebelles', Associated Press, 28 November 2007.

41   Merchet, Jean-Dominique, *Libération*, 23 March 2007.

42   Wood, Graeme, *Foreign Policy*, Issue 180, July–August 2010.

43   www.linternaute.com

44   www.afrik.com

45   www.diplomatie.gouv.fr

46   www.cellulefrancafrique.org

47   www.cellulefrancafrique.org

48   www.lexpress.fr

49   *Central African Republic: Anatomy of a Phantom State*, Crisis Group Africa Report N° 136, 13 December 2007.

50   Crisis Group interview, Paris, June 2007.

Peter Baxter is an author, amateur historian and African field, mountain and heritage travel guide. Born in Kenya, Peter has lived and travelled over much of southern and central Africa. He was educated in Rhodesia (Zimbabwe), leaving the country after independence for an extended bout of travel before returning in 1989. Since then he has guided in all the major mountain ranges south of the equator, helping develop the concept of sustainable travel, and the touring of battlefield and heritage sites in East Africa. Peter lives in the United States, working on marketing African heritage travel as well as a variety of book projects. His interests include British Imperial history in Africa and the East Africa campaign of the First World War in particular. He is married with three children.

The publishers extend a special thank-you to Yves Debay of *Assaut* magazine, who went the extra mile in supplying many of the high-quality photos that appear in this publication.